ACCESSING M

ENHANCING STUDENT LEARNING IN THE GENERAL MUSIC CLASSROOM USING UDL

Kimberly McCord — Amy Gruben — Jesse Rathgeber

Alfred Music
P.O. Box 10003
Van Nuys, CA 91410-0003
alfred.com

ISBN-10: 1-4706-1901-4
ISBN-13: 978-1-4706-1901-3

Cover Art
Crashed Color by Ella Zona

Table of Contents

Acknowledgements

Thank you to the following teachers for testing our ideas and giving us feedback: Donna Zawatski, Leah Crews, Maria Gandara, Nancy O'Neill, and Lauren Bernacki.

Introduction

Universal Design began as a result of the first laws that required buildings to be accessible for people with disabilities in the mid-1970s. Architects decided it was more cost efficient to design buildings that were naturally accessible than to add on wheelchair ramps and other accommodations for people who might use public buildings. The same concept can be applied to education. Teachers write lesson plans, but what happens if a new student who joins an ensemble happens to be blind? If the teacher has been teaching music from notation, he or she may have to figure out some alternative activities or outside help for our new student. Music can be exclusionary or awkward for students with disabilities who want to participate without feeling singled out or different from their peers who may notice they aren't learning the same way. Universal Design for Learning (UDL) is a way of planning, teaching, and assessing instruction that is naturally inclusive of all possible types of learners. And guess what? In the process, typical learners will learn better, too, because they are being taught with more flexibility.

The three main principles of UDL to be considered when designing lessons are: 1) multiple means of representation, 2) multiple means of action and expression, and 3) multiple means of engagement. This requires the teacher to be flexible and to think about what is most important that the student understands from the lesson. If it is rondo form, the different ways to represent rondo form should be considered (listening, playing, or singing a piece in rondo form, moving, or composing). Representing the concept through different learning modes (aural, visual, and kinesthetic/ tactile) could help engage all learners. Teachers tend to teach primarily through their own preferred learning modes. A teacher may be a visual learner who writes on the board, uses visuals, and even uses language that is visually descriptive. He or she may have classroom students who learn better if they have new information verbally explained or if they pat rhythms on thighs. Typical students do better when concepts are presented through different learning modes, but a student with vision loss is going to especially need teachers who make heavy use of visuals to represent concepts through their stronger learning modes (aural and kinesthetic/tactile).

Students, such as those who are nonverbal, need flexibility in how they demonstrate their understanding of what has been taught. The first national standard for music education states that all students should be able to sing alone and with others. If a student can't sing because she has a communication disorder, how can teachers assess her in regards to matching pitch? There are many ways flexible UDL teachers can assess in this situation: student demonstrations of the correct Curwen hand signs for *sol* and *mi*, for example. A student who is hard of hearing might demonstrate pitch matching through written notation rather than voiced singing.

Finally, differentiated instruction requires teachers to know their students well and think about how to best engage them. Many students with Asperger Syndrome have passionate interests in specific areas. For example, if a student loves maps and collects roadway signs, he might more easily remember the that *fine* means stop if given a visual of a stop sign drawn around the word, as will all the other students in the class! A student with Attention Deficit Disorder might be more successful during a long rehearsal if he is allowed two seats in the classroom and permission to get up and move between the two seats. Allowing students choice and empowering them to advocate for their own best learning are valuable tools for success in the world. Students who are engaged and aware of their abilities and learning needs are more easily able to advocate for themselves—this is *self-determination*, a very important skill students with disabilities need to learn.

At the end of this book are lists of helpful resources. At the top of the list for all UDL users is the Center for Applied Special Technology (CAST) website at http:// www.cast.org. The book written by UDL gurus David H. Rose and Anne Meyer, *Teaching Every Student in the Digital Age: Universal Design for Learning* (2002), is even available to read, free of charge, on the website. Much of the book is actually presented in multiple ways so that people with a variety of disabilities can easily access it.

As music teachers, the three of us have encountered students at all age levels occasionally struggling with participation in music ensembles and classes. The strategies, examples, and visuals in this book are offered because they have worked with our students and the students of various teachers who have also tested and tried them out. We hope this will be a starting place for you to explore alternative ways to reach the students in your classrooms with disabilities.

Amy Gruben, Kimberly McCord, and Jesse Rathgeber

Multiple Means of Engagement

Flexibility in ways the teacher engages students helps to include all learners in the lesson and enables fair assessments. Hammel and Hourigan (2011) remind music teachers that "fair is not always equal." To engage and assess students with disabilities requires music teachers to first examine what is most important to learn. Then, they must find different ways students can be motivated to engage in learning and different ways to tell if learning occurred.

For example, if the lesson is focused on *sol* and *mi*, different ways students can demonstrate that they understand *sol* and *mi* should be considered. Singing does not need to be the only way; this gives the music teacher flexibility in ways to engage the student to recognize the two pitches. Singing is obviously one way, but hand signs would be another, as would pushing buttons to activate a recording of a voice singing *sol* and *mi*.

Teachers may take exception with allowing some students options that could be perceived as easier, keeping in mind that "fair is not always equal." For example, a student with a learning disability who struggles with fluent music reading should not be assessed on fluent music reading. Instead, other ways to engage and assess the student who is beginning to master names of the notes on the lines and spaces of the staff should be considered—all students should not be required to identify similar and different phrases, this assumes students are able to analyze both pitch and rhythm.

Students who have difficulty writing should be allowed to use a computer instead or to circle words or images to identify correct answers.

Presenting visuals of song lyrics can be helpful for visual learners. Limiting these visuals to only the words and not the notation can help students process the words more easily. Students with hearing loss may find difficulty trying to learn a song by watching an interpreter and the music teacher at the same time—"Hmm, was that word 'tap' or 'pat'?" Tracking the words with a finger or a pointer, and including images for important ones, could help support emerging readers. If the first verse is about head and shoulders, an image should show the two body parts. Verse two for knees and ankles should show those two body parts. Teachers can earn big points with their administrations for supporting literacy, and all students will have the words to reference as well.

Instructions should be given facing the class so that lip readers can see the teacher's mouth, and anything that is presented visually should be verbally described to include students with vision loss. Visuals can be supplemented with tactile objects, such as balls with different surfaces to represent form, instrument sounds, etc.

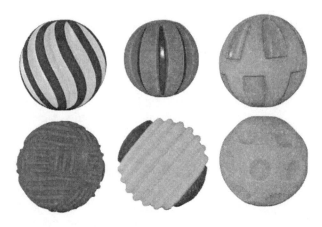

If playing recorders bothers the hearing of students with sensory disorders, they may be given permission to wear noise-cancelling headphones or earplugs, or even sit in a beanbag chair away from the rest of the class and play their part on a Skoog or an iPad. Likewise, if playing certain instruments with high, ringing pitches bothers these students, they should not be asked to play the instruments, and should be allowed to sit away from the instruments when others play them. If students cover their ears or roll up into a ball like the child in the photo below, it is a cue to the teacher that the instrument is irritating to them. In this case, it is the glockenspiel.

Holding hands when dancing with a partner is another activity that is hard for some children with autism. Instead, each partner can hold one end of a chopstick; it will keep contact without touching.

The general music classroom is an exciting multi-sensory learning environment, but it can easily become too stimulating for some students. Having a beanbag chair in an isolated section of the classroom offers a quiet place for students to go as needed. Children with emotional and behavioral disorders or sensory integration disorder will appreciate a place to get away from the overstimulation of the music classroom.

Puppets are an excellent way to engage all children but are especially motivating to children on the autism spectrum and students with attention difficulties. Echo singing to a parrot puppet is more engaging for some children than making eye contact and singing to the teacher. Puppets and stuffed animals can help support joint attention, which means looking at what others are looking at. This is often an IEP goal for students with autism, singing to a puppet or hitting a hand drum when cued is a powerful way to encourage development of joint attention.

Multiple Means of Representing Symbolic Systems

Notation

One of the biggest challenges for students participating in music is the emphasis placed on the importance of musical literacy. In many great musical cultures and genres, music is never notated. Many of the greatest jazz musicians, including much of the early Count Basie band, did not read music fluently, yet they continued to be the standard for a swinging band.

When teachers insist on students reading music, they essentially eliminate all of the talented musicians who might be wonderful improvisers, creative interpreters, and playful collaborators. Many students with disabilities will struggle with reading music, some will not be able to read at all, and others will never be fluent readers. These students will learn best by ear. Supplying recordings ahead of time so parts can be learned aurally can be effective. If possible, the part should be isolated on a recording with a like instrument or voice in the same octave.

Reading music involves very sophisticated processing. Children who are just starting to learn band instruments have to remember how to hold them, how to form an embouchure, how to tongue properly, the key signature and meter—and on top of that they are expected to be able to read music that relies on processing pitch, rhythm, articulations, and dynamics all at the same time! That is an awful lot to process at once. This book presents some examples of ways to adapt notation for students that may help struggling readers keep up.

Jesse Rathgeber has developed several ways to adapt notation to help students with music reading challenges. Some examples are inspired by adapted notation ideas from Chris Lapka. "Hot Cross Buns" seems to be one piece that everyone encounters sooner or later. What follows is a series of different ways to represent notation for recorder. Additional examples are provided at the end of the book in Appendix A for "Twinkle, Twinkle, Little Star," "Hey, Ho, Nobody Home," "Yankee Doodle," and "Amazing Grace."

First, here is "Hot Cross Buns" in traditional notation:

Hot Cross Buns

Now here it is with added numbers to help students remember how many fingers cover the top three holes of the recorder:

"Hot Cross Buns" with the names of the notes displayed in different colors. This helps some students to see the names better.

Allowing students to label their notes is not "cheating" and is not a "crutch," but a way they can adapt the notation to be functional for themselves.

Recorder fingerings have been placed above each note:

Hot Cross Buns

Iconic notation displays the duration and pitch of notation:

Hot Cross Buns

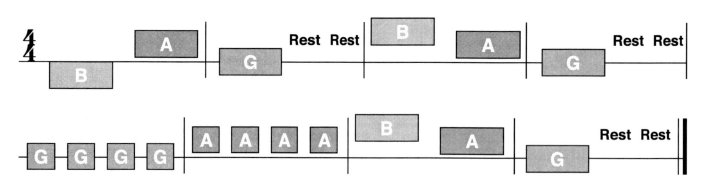

Glovert-style notation is similar, only duration is represented by size of the letters.

Hot Cross Buns

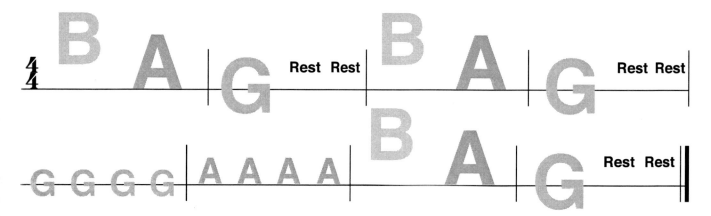

Lapka, C. (2006). Students with disabilities in high school band:"We can do it!". *Music Educators Journal*, 92(4), 105-106.

Color-dot notation shows traditional notation with highlighted dots in color that represent duration.

Hot Cross Buns

Stem names use ties to show duration.

Hot Cross Buns

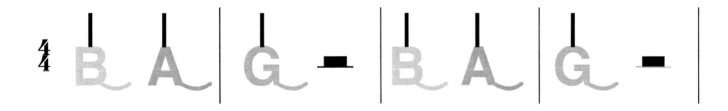

Caution About Using Color

Before using colors with classes, the teacher should determine if there are students with color blindness in the class. If so, the student should be provided with a black-and-white page. Generally, black background with white printing is the easiest to see.

Manipulatives

Many students with disabilities have accommodations written into their IEPs that recommend the use of manipulatives. One way to show notation using an easy-to-make system is this example made with building toys or Legos™. The green board represents a measure in 4/4 time and the blocks show one combination of notes and rests to create four beats.

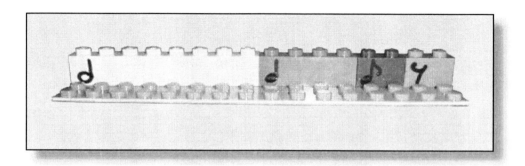

Signs that have "beat" written on one side and "rhythm" on the other are a good way for all students to show they can hear when a beat is performed as opposed to a rhythm.

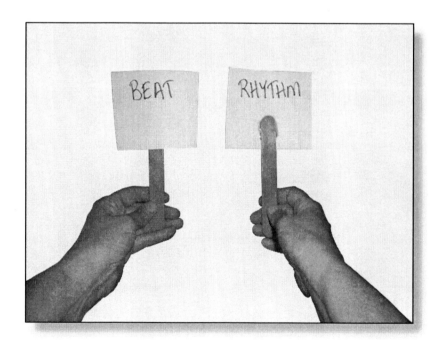

Finale™ notation software has several education templates for representing notation in other forms. Boomwhacker notation displays note heads in the colors of Boomwhackers™.

Finale™ Boomwhacker® Example

Boomwhacker® Tubes

Finale™ Alphanotes display names of notes in their note heads.

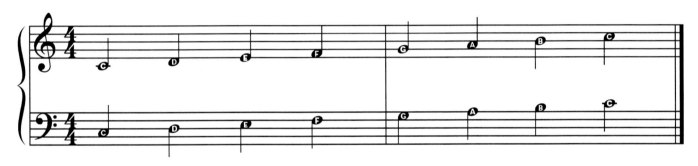

Finale™ Alphanote Solfège displays solfège in the note heads.

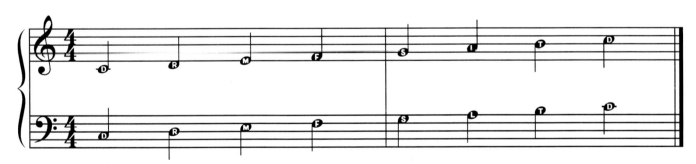

Making note heads larger is another way to help all students differentiate notes. Finale™ and Sibelius™ both have this capability.

Figurenotes is a system that was developed by Kaarlo Uusitalo in Finland for teaching notation to individuals with intellectual disabilities. An excellent English tutorial is located at the Drake Music Scotland website: http://www.drakemusic.org/sites/drakemusic. org/files/Introducing-Figurenotes.pdf

Solfège

Solfège was developed by Guido d'Arezzo (990–1050) to denote pitches. The Curwen Hand Signs are a system developed by the Rev. John Spencer Curwen (1816–1880) to show solfège syllables, using one or two hands against the body to denote pitch levels and placement. Hand signs can be shown in color.

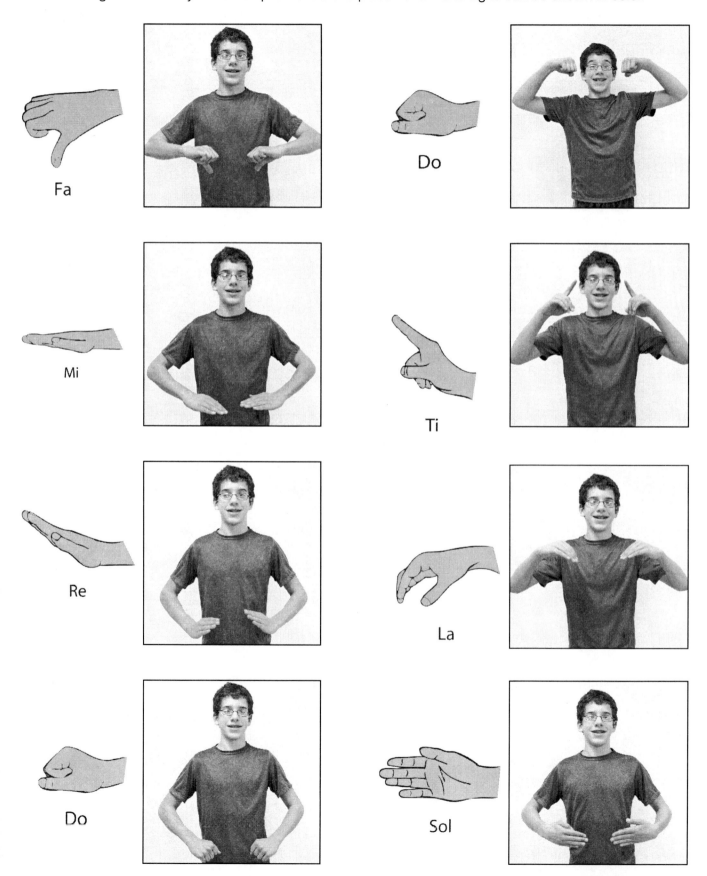

Hand Staff

A hand staff is a wonderful UDL way for students to experience the staff.
Here is a visual that will help to support visual learners.

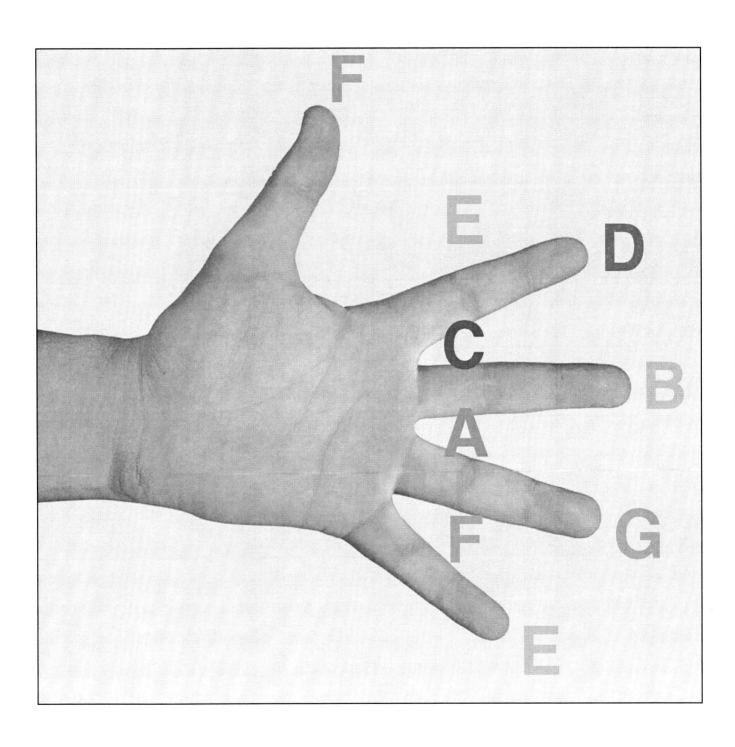

Solfège on the Keyboard

Piano diagrams are useful for students who are just learning to play the keyboard. Sometimes, providing too much information (such as an entire keyboard map) overwhelms students who are navigating a difficult terrain of white and black keys. Using a keyboard diagram that highlights only the notes that students use makes the song easier to process, particularly for students with intellectual disabilities. Alternately, teachers can use label stickers and place them directly on the keys that are to be played. These are easily removable with a little adhesive remover. If a student needs more tactile sensation, taping a small piece of felt to the first key of the song can be effective. When demonstrating the music, the teacher sings and plays the song multiple ways, using solfège, scale degrees, and pitches. Often, students have a preferred method of learning amongst these tools. Taking an informal survey of which method students like best can help them to feel confident in their learning modality and proud of the individual ways they learn. It's important to continually emphasize that different learning styles are to be celebrated.

Teaching keyboarding color visuals can be simple.

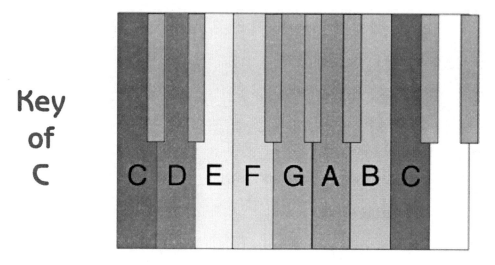

Pitches may also be shown with solfège on scale degree numbers.

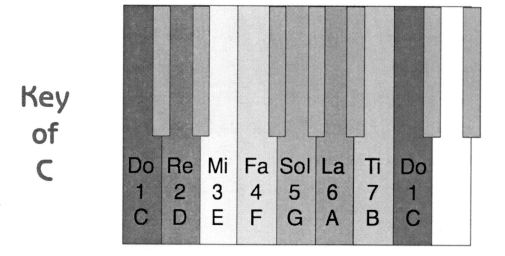

Additional examples in the keys of G and D may be found in Appendix B.

Tablature

Hot Cross Buns

Some students experience difficulty reversing fingering charts and other visuals that appear differently than the way the instrument looks from the students' point of view. Upside-down tablature solves this by being more intuitive to the student.

Standard Notation

Upside-Down Tablature

Guitar

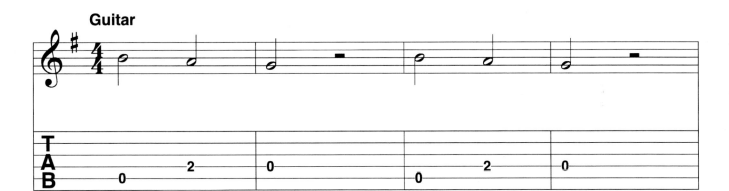

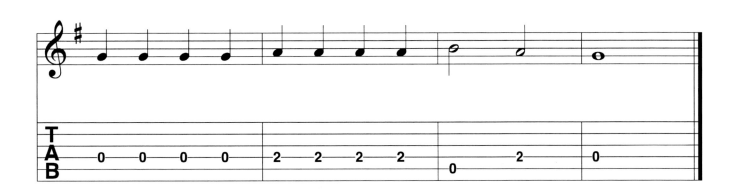

The above example does not include lyrics. If lyrics aren't necessary, teachers can display only what students need to see to help reduce frustration with trying to process so much. When more than one line of music is presented at a time (a score or lyrics), it will tend to slow down most students' (typical and those with disabilities) reading fluency.

Hot Cross Buns

Standard Notation

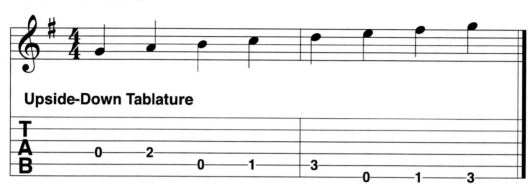

Upside-Down Tablature

Guitar

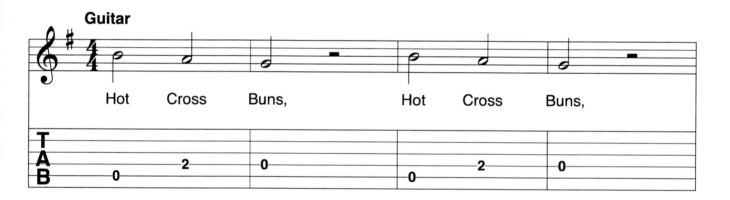

Hot   Cross   Buns,   Hot   Cross   Buns,

One a pen - ny, Two a pen - ny, Hot   Cross   Buns.

Additional tablature examples may be found in Appendix C.

Rhythm Blocks

Rhythm reading and notating can be difficult for many students. The included rhythm notation blocks allow students to actually see the durational values of each rhythm symbol in relation to other symbols. A teacher might represent a rhythm for sight-reading in both traditional and rhythm block form as to allow students another level of visual support. Also, when printed out, students can make use of the rhythm blocks as physical manipulatives to notate their own rhythms or to represent standard notated rhythms in a manner more fitting to their learning styles.

Rhythm Block Manipulatives

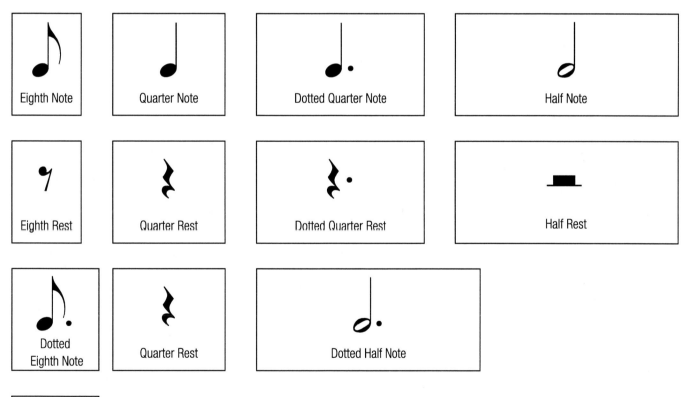

Rhythm Block Manipulatives

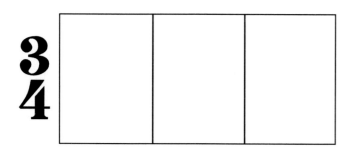

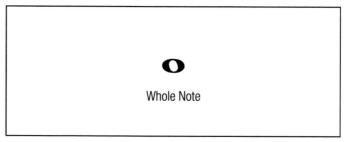

Whole Note

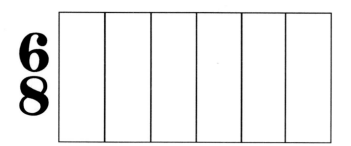

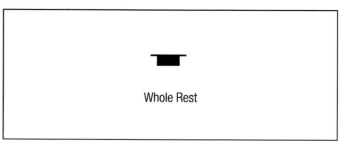

Whole Rest

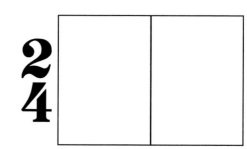

Orff

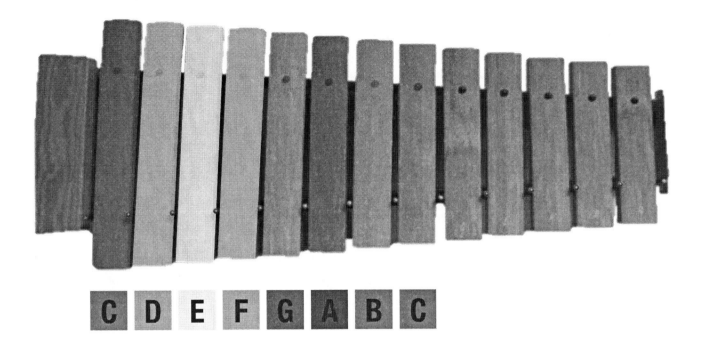

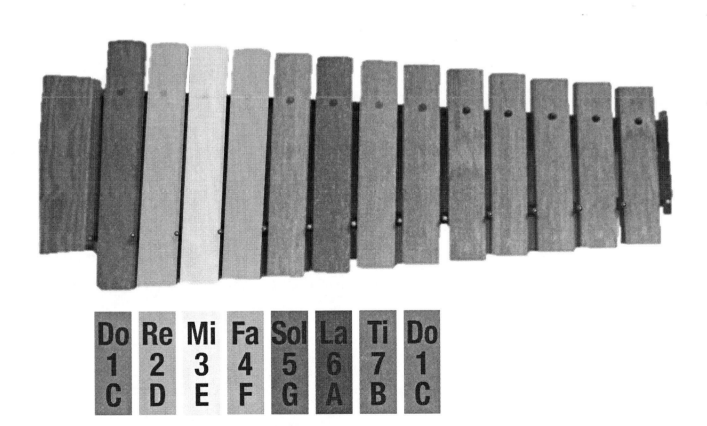

Strategies for Using Orff Instruments with Students Who Have Disabilities

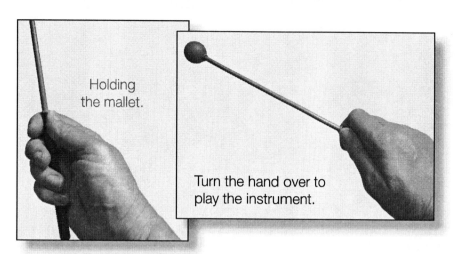

Holding the mallet.

Turn the hand over to play the instrument.

Play the bars in the center for the best sound and let the mallet bounce back up from each bar.

If unused bars are removed and the others are grouped together in the middle, students with vision loss and physical disabilities will be more successful playing cross-over borduns and other parts.

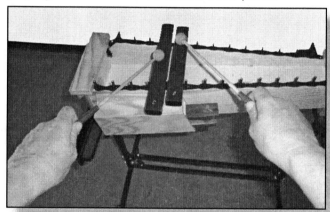

When teaching visually impaired students who read Braille, the vision teacher can create Braille stickers of pitch names and put them on bar edges to help orient students to pitches.

Students with hearing loss are most successful on the lowest-pitched Orff instruments, because residual hearing is most often present in the low frequencies. When playing the contrabass bars, students should be encouraged to put a hand on the side of the box or lean a knee against the box to feel the vibrations. This will help them to know how loud they are playing.

Fingering Charts

Fingering charts are often represented showing the image of the instrument, as it would look if someone else held the instrument reversed in front of the student. Many students have difficulty translating this image to what they see when they hold the instrument in playing position. Fingering charts that are represented from the students' playing position and perspective are much easier to read and understand.

Recorder

The recorder charts are shown with fingerings and notation. First fingers are in red, second fingers are in blue, third fingers are in orange, and fourth fingers are in purple. The thumb is shown with a "T" in brown (see data disk for color). Another version is the upside-down image as it looks from the player's perspective. Black dots represent covered holes, and brackets show holes covered by each hand. Brackets are positioned so they imitate fingers attached to the hand.

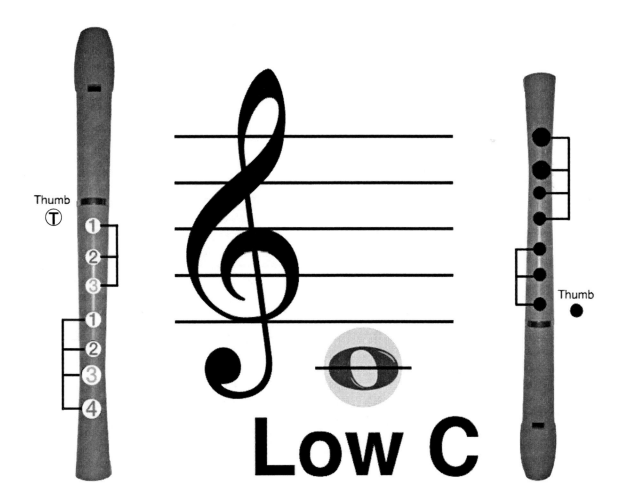

Low C

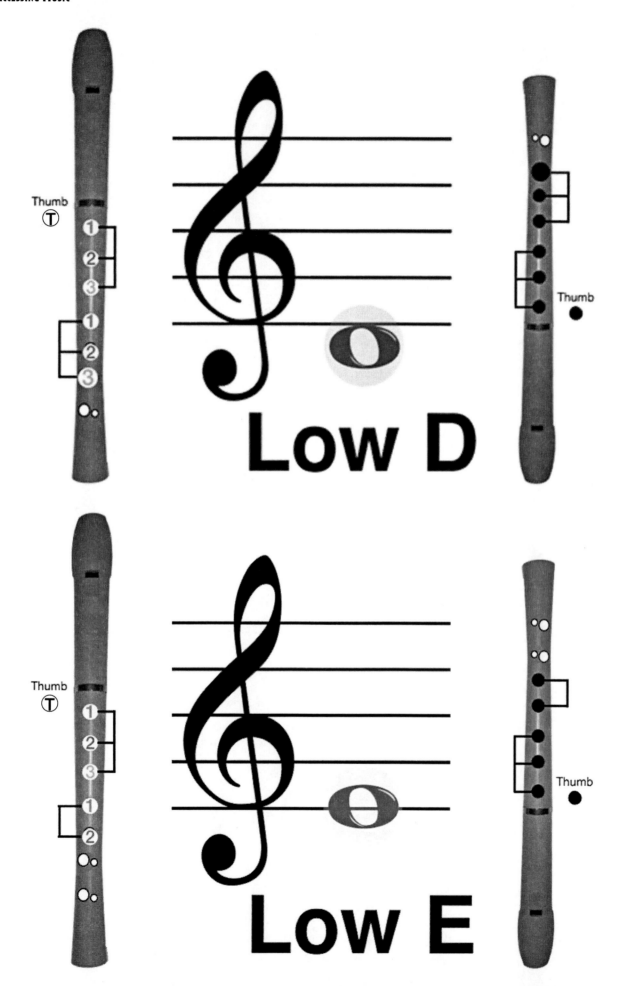

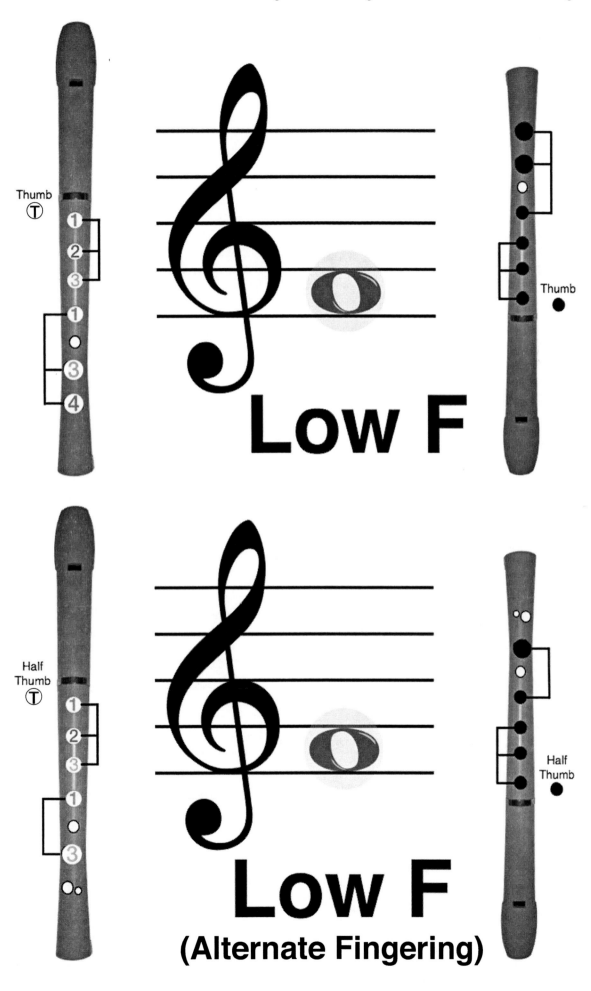

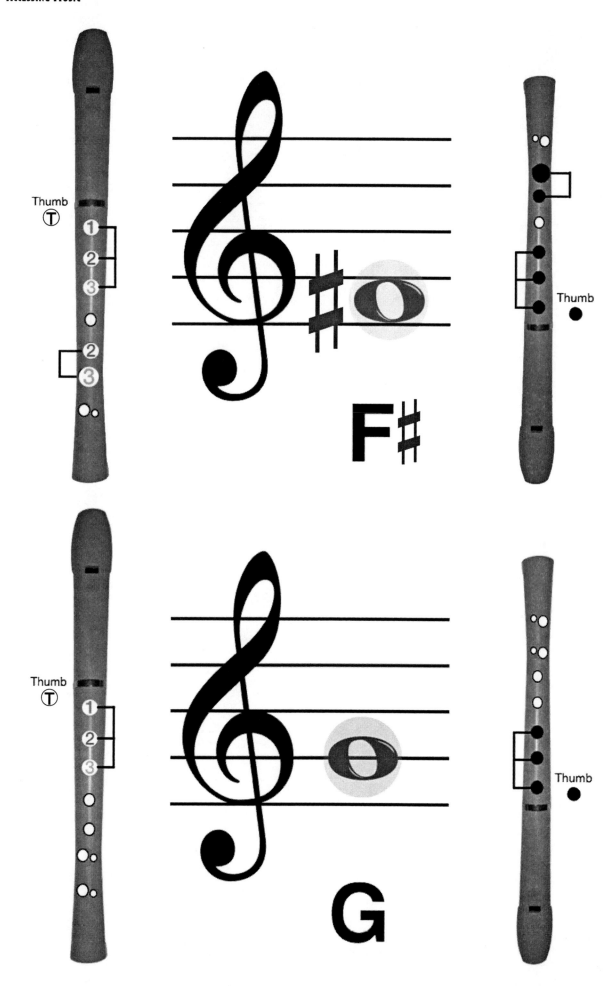

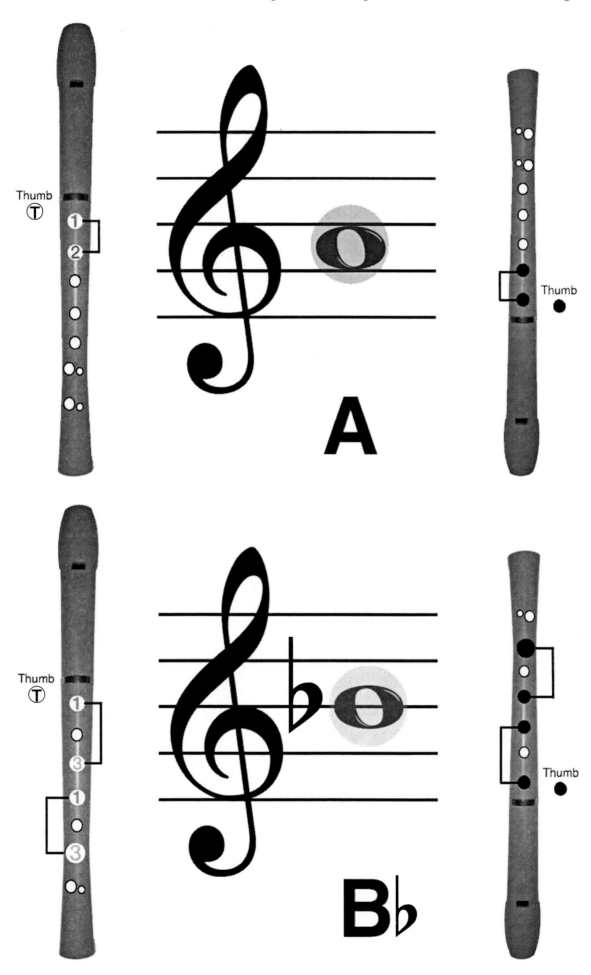

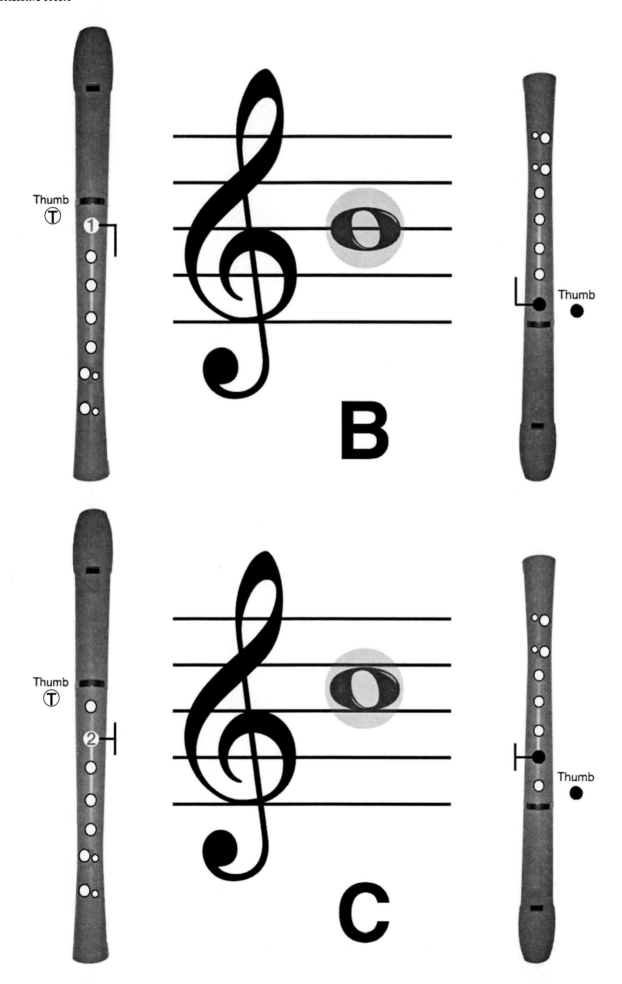

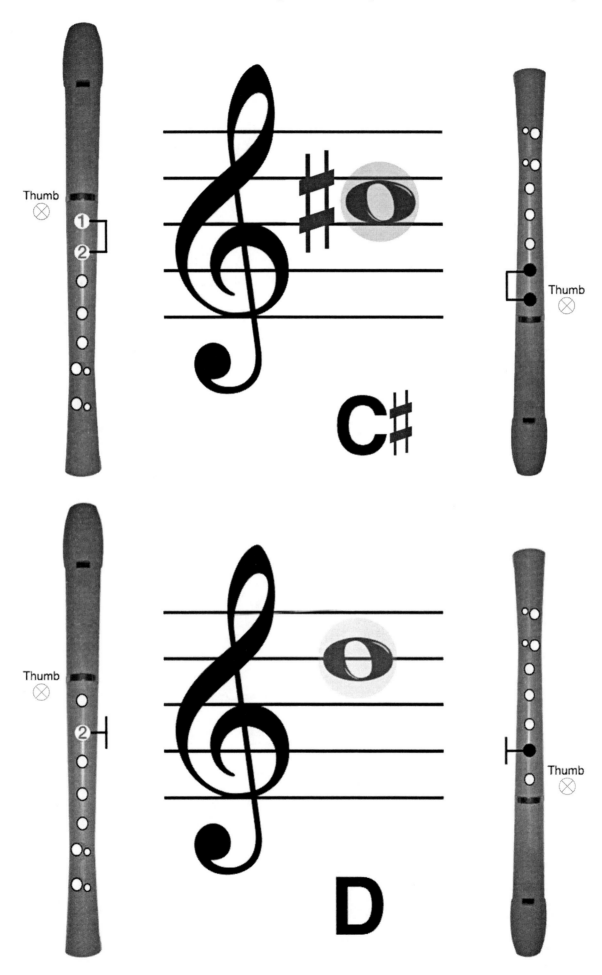

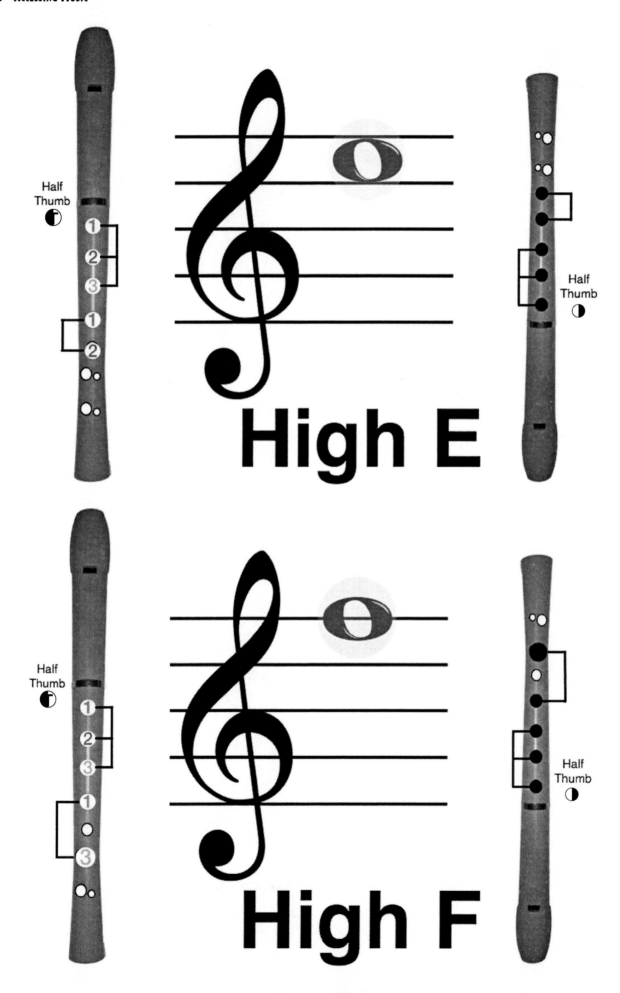

Half
Thumb

High E

Half
Thumb

Half
Thumb

High F

Half
Thumb

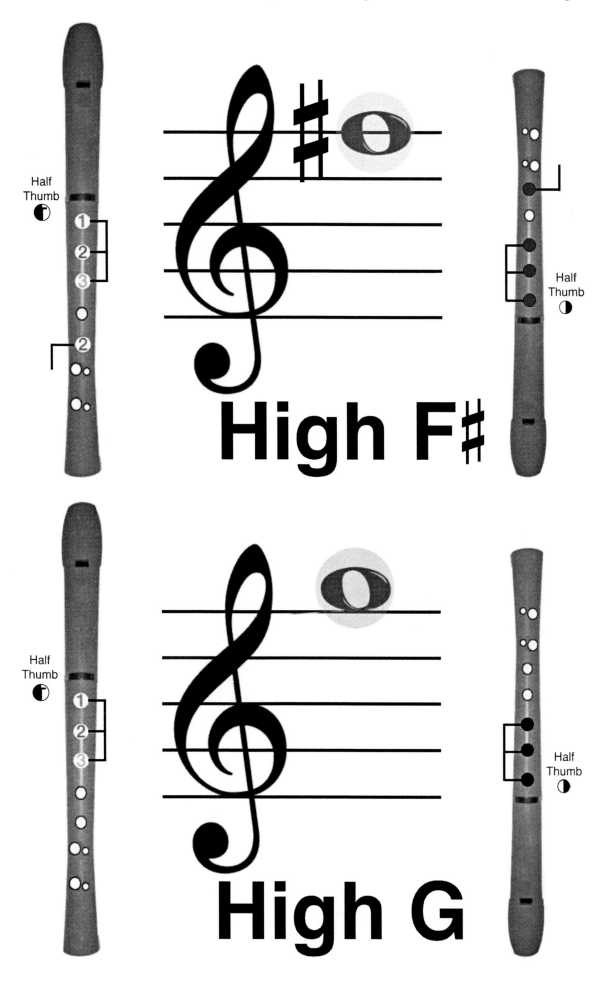

Ukulele

Ukulele is becoming very popular in general music classes. Its size and easy fingerings make it very accessible for students with disabilities. Color-coded fingering charts that are photographed from the player's perspective are included below for the commonly used chords.

To adapt these visual charts for students with vision loss or tactile learners, the vision teacher can print the chart (not the photograph) on their special printer. It will raise the ink and create an embossed effect that will enable students to touch the chart and feel the image.

In relation to the backward Tab shown in the notation section, pictures demonstrating instrument fingerings from the view of holding the instrument to play can be more intuitive for beginning musicians.

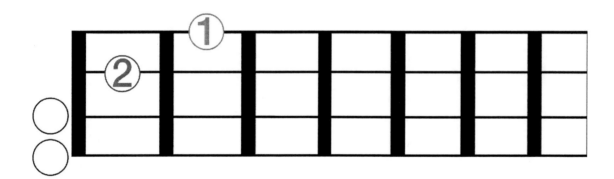

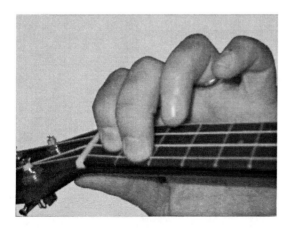

A
A Major

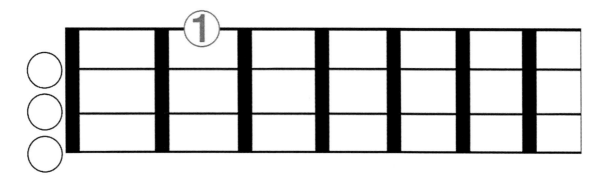

Am
A minor

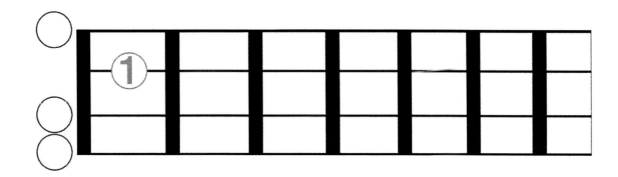

A7
A Dominant 7th

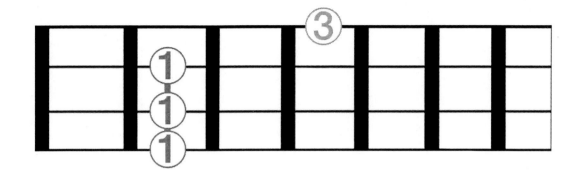

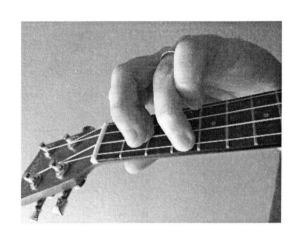

Bm
B minor

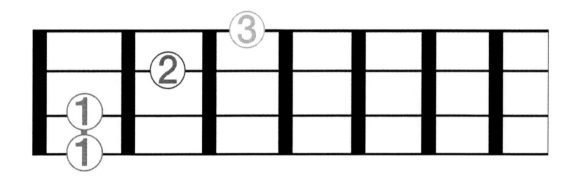

B♭
B♭ Major

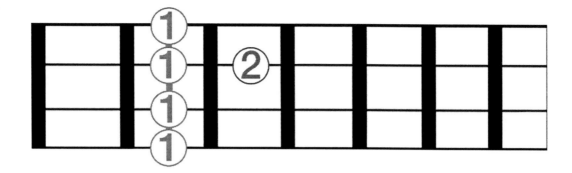

B7
B Dominant 7th

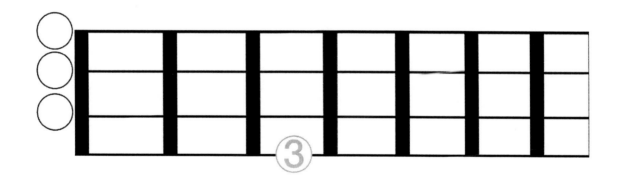

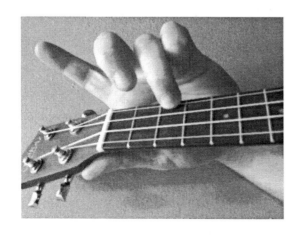

C
C Major

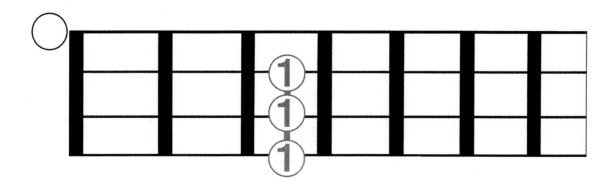

Cm
C minor

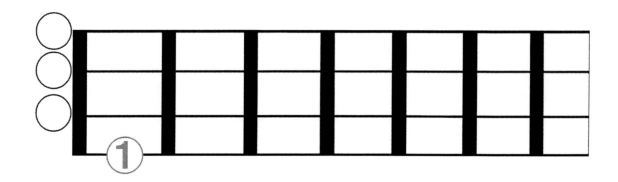

C7
C Dominant 7th

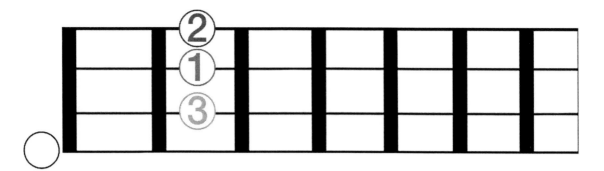

D
D Major

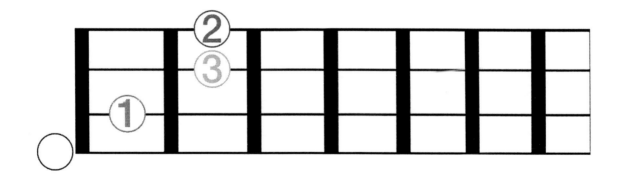

Dm
D minor

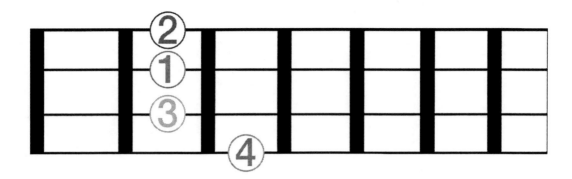

D7
D Dominant 7th

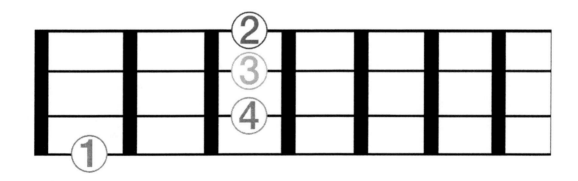

E
E Major

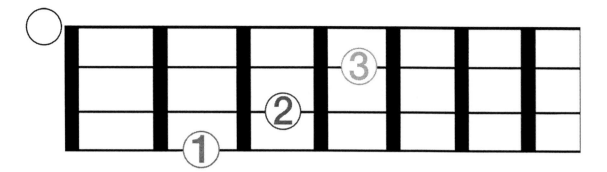

Em
E minor

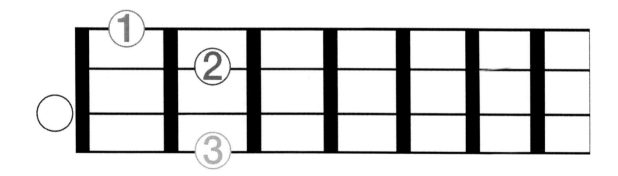

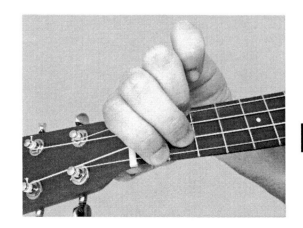

E7
E Dominant 7th

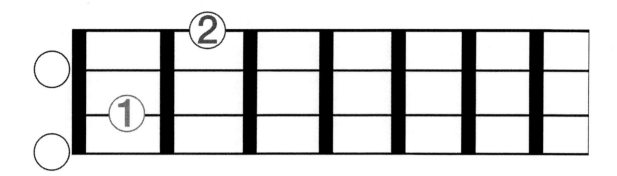

F
F Major

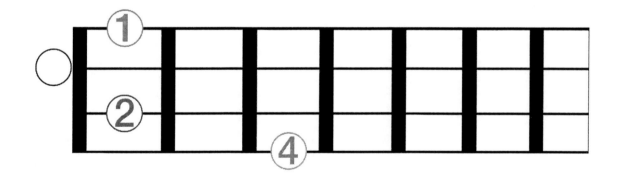

Fm
F minor

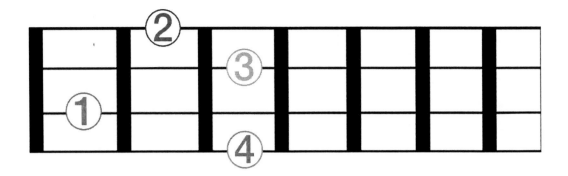

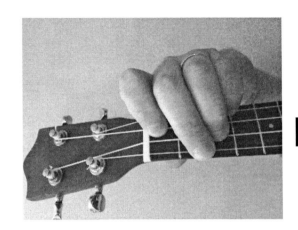

F7
F Dominant 7th

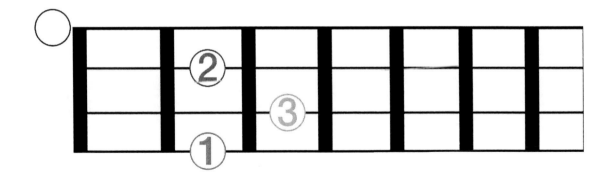

G
G Major

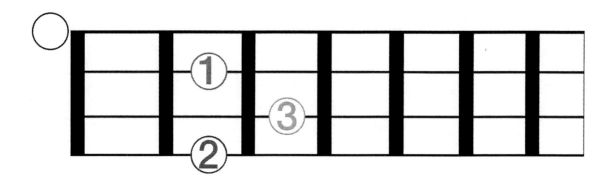

G
G Major
alternate fingering

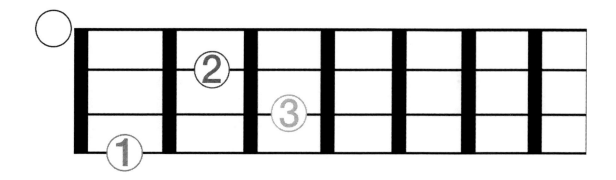

Gm
G minor

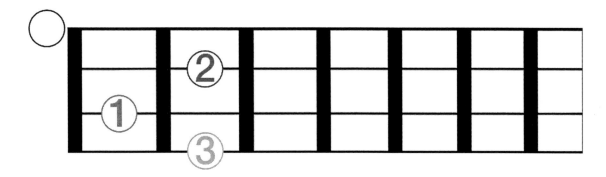

G7

G Dominant 7th

Guitar

Guitar fingering charts typically display the neck of the guitar straight up and down, as if someone was holding a guitar out toward the student. However, when one plays the guitar, the guitar is tilted on its side and not straight up and down. These re-imagined guitar charts help students better visualize how to finger chords while staying in the proper playing position. The chart acts as a mirror of the student's hand: If a note is to be played on the High E String, it will be shown on the bottom line of the chart, in accordance with where High E is played as one strums the guitar. The corresponding pictures are also designed to line up with how students see themselves as they play. They are taken from the angle of looking down at one's hand from above, the exact view students will experience as they learn to finger new chords.

Traditional guitar tablature can be unintuitive for students who do not read standard notation or are still developing their notation-reading skills. When students hold the guitar to play, the highest pitches are on the strings physically closest to the floor. However, traditional guitar tablature represents the highest string on the highest line of the figure. Upside-down guitar tablature notates the pitches in a way that mirrors the musician. If a note is to be played on the lowest physical string, it is notated on the lowest line of the upside down tablature. For many young guitar students, upside down tablature can turn music reading right side up.

This adaptation has been particularly useful in classrooms for both students on the autism spectrum and students with intellectual disabilities. Usually, using upside down tablature is enough support for students with autism. Sometimes, though, students need more modification. Teachers can use a set of highlighters to show students how to highlight notes on each string in different colors. Any note on the first string is highlighted in yellow and any note on the second string is highlighted in blue, for instance. The teachers can help their students complete an example piece, and then they are typically able to use the color system to continue on their own for subsequent musical pieces. This has the added benefit of teaching musical independence and the ways in which professional musicians mark their own music. Occasionally, a student might feel silly needing to support their notation reading in this manner. In those cases, the teacher might take out their own well-marked scores for conducting and performing. The student's highlighted music will look pristine next to these dog-eared and scribbled-on octavos!

When using this adaptation for students with profound intellectual disabilities, it is best to use the above strategies but also remove any lines from the tablature that the students are not using. For example, when students learn a song that utilizes only the first and second strings, the student's tablature would display only two lines. If a teacher is in the lucky position of having a guitar assigned to just one special needs student, one might string the guitar as the student learns. If the teacher introduces melodies starting on the first string and then advances to more difficult melodies and chords, the guitar could start with only having one string. As the student mastered a string, another could be added to the guitar. In this way, students would have no confusion on which string they were to play.

Common guitar chords are represented on the following pages.

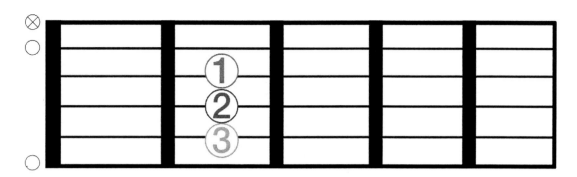

A
A Major

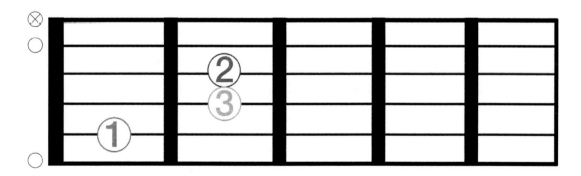

Am
A minor

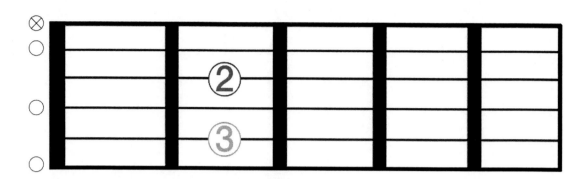

A7
A Dominant 7th

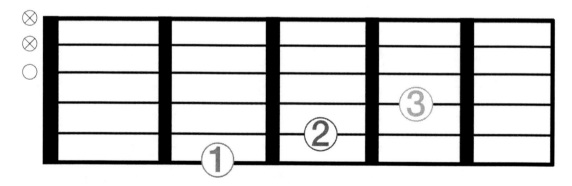

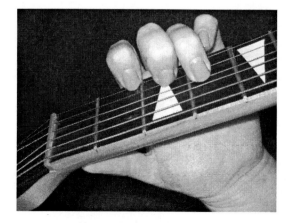

Bm
B minor

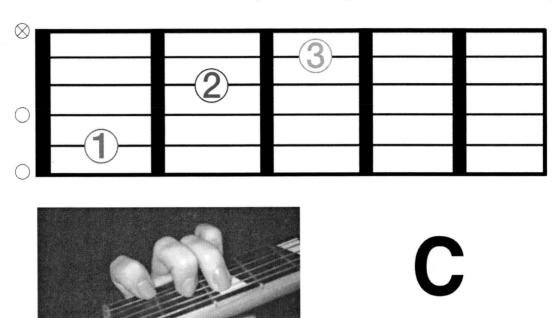

C
C Major

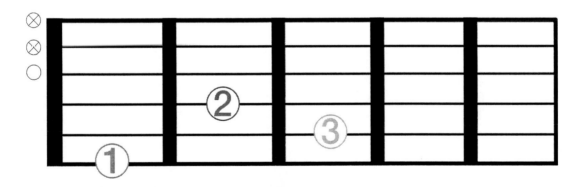

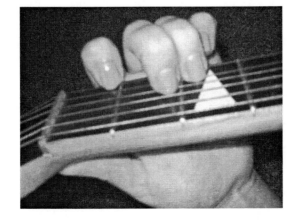

Dm
D minor

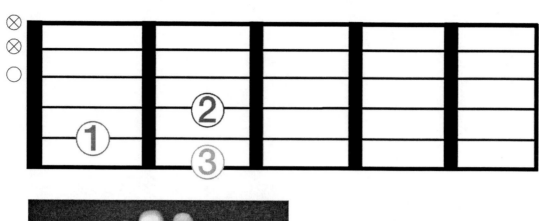

D7
D Dominant 7th

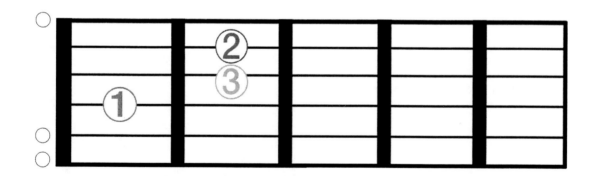

E
E Major

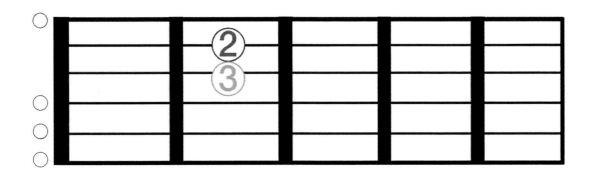

Em
E minor

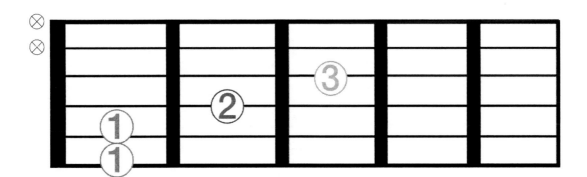

F
F Major

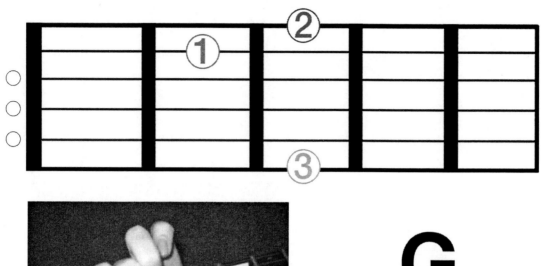

G
G Major

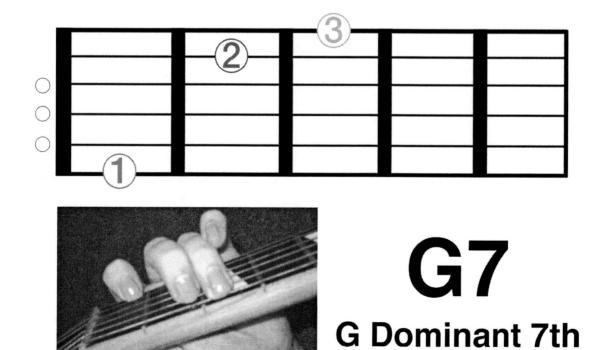

G7
G Dominant 7th

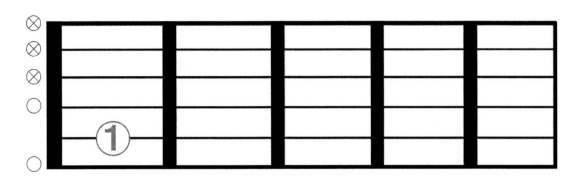

C
C Major
Quick Fingering

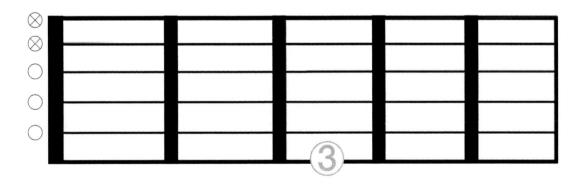

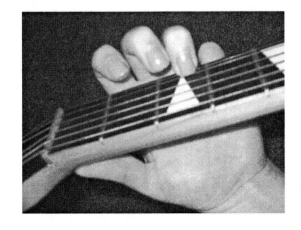

G
G Major
Quick Fingering

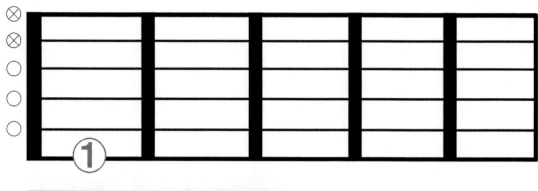

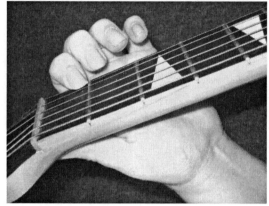

G7
G Dominant 7th
Quick Fingering

Open Tuning for Guitar

When teaching guitar to a student who has limited muscle strength in their hands or fingers, a teacher may consider utilizing an open tuning method. In an open tuning method, the guitar is re-tuned from its standard E-B-G-D-A-E to another chord, such as C or G. In open G tuning, for example, the guitar's strings would be tuned to D-B-G-D-B-D. When using this tuning, students are able to still play a full chord (G) without pressing any frets. Other chords can easily be achieved by barring the other strings. More information about this method can be found in *The Green Songbook* (Alfred Music).

Small plastic or wooden tubes (similar to a short dowel rod) that have a handle attached can be used to easily bar all the strings at once with an open tuning method. It has been used with great success with severely physically disabled students, and is especially effective with the help of a classroom aide.

Visuals

Listening maps are typically created for visual learners to follow. Students who rely on aural and kinesthetic/tactile learning modes may find listening maps difficult or impossible to follow. Vision teachers can use the raised text copy machine to turn listening maps into tactile maps. This can also be done with puff paint. Complex images will not translate well, but lines and simple objects can be followed with assistance from a paraprofessional.

Large tactile listening maps that fit on music stands may be created that can be read from left to right as the recording plays. Below is an example of Mussorgsky's "Ballet of the Unhatched Chicks" from *Pictures at an Exhibition*.

Tactile listening maps can be created from puff paint, pieces of foam, buttons, or just about any object that can be easily felt.

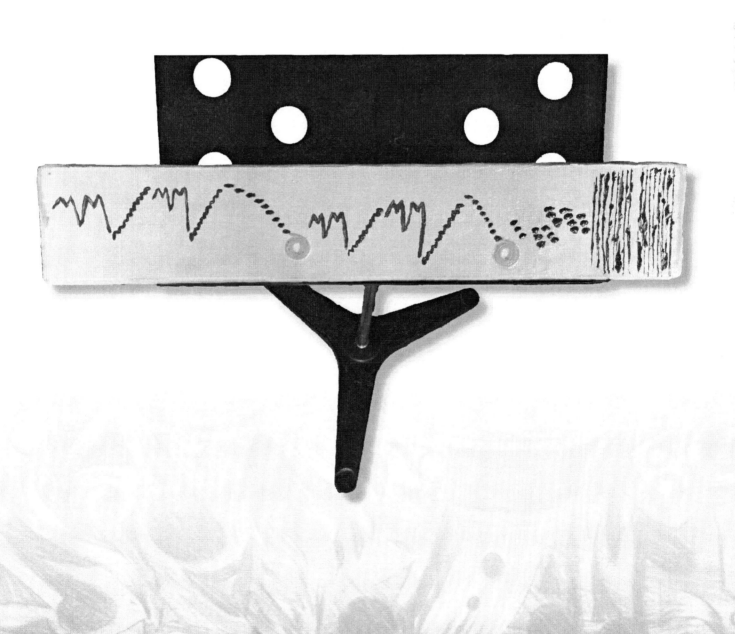

Signs of Struggle with Reading Notation, Fingering Charts, and Visuals

Students with specified learning disabilities in reading and math will likely be the ones who struggle the most with processing visual information. Often, very creative and gifted musicians have learning disabilities that impact music reading. When these students are gifted in one or more areas, they are called **twice exceptional**.

Some types of learning disabilities do not seem to impact music reading, whereas others do. For example, dyslexia can affect ability to see notes in the proper places on the staff. Special educators use highlighters to help students with this problem when reading words. Music teachers can highlight spaces on the staff, as this helps students to better anchor the notes to the proper place. Erasable highlighters are convenient for school-owned music. There are also highlighter strips that work like whiteout strips, but they are a bit more cumbersome to use. Below is a highlighted music staff (see data disk for color).

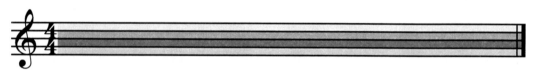

Often students who struggle with processing music notation will write the names of the notes underneath the notes to help them compensate. It is beneficial to praise students when they write note names rather than the opposite, common response, which is to tell them to erase the names to prevent dependency on writing these out. Students do this as a way to adapt the music for their own learning needs—this is a good thing!

Reading everything quickly will be difficult. In conversations with musicians with learning disabilities, they relate that what they focus on first is pitches, then rhythm, and then articulations and dynamics. They also tend to use their ears to listen to others model the rhythm and memorize it instead of trying to process counting. Students with rhythmic challenges are often receiving support in math classes; their particular type of learning disability is called dyscalculia. It is difficult for them to quickly process abstract symbols. Providing a recording of their part or a very strong aural example in class will help.

Sometimes students follow teachers' fingers rather than reading the music. This is another way students compensate when reading music is too overwhelming. Encouraging them to do this and letting them play with a strong partner they can watch for a good example can be effective.

Pairing students on an instrument is a good idea. This allows a student who needs extra time to process the music to watch the other person model the playing first, before he or she tries it. When teaching the Orff process, the practice of performing rhythms on body percussion before transferring to instruments is an excellent way to support students who need extra processing time.

Although Braille music notation, a system that uses a sequence of raised dots to represent music, is excellent, it does not work well for a student who is playing an instrument, because the student has to use hands to read the music and then transfer it to the instrument. It also requires a teacher who understands the system to teach it well. Musicians with vision loss prefer to learn by rote or by listening to recordings.

If students say they don't like an instrument or music class, it is often because they experience frustration in music class. Determining which activities cause the problem can lead to solutions.

Multiple Means of Action and Expression

Multiple Means for Experiencing Musical Concepts

Musical elements and concepts can be organized like the Music Concepts Chart below:

Music Concept Chart

Elements of Music	Definitions	Music Concepts
Timbre	The unique tone color of a voice instrument or sound source	• Environmental • Vocal • Instrumental
Expressive Qualities *Dynamics* *Tempo* *Articulation*	 The degree of loudness or softness of music The speed of a piece of music The manner in which musical tones are played (attacked) in performance	• soft/loud • gradual softer or louder • fast/slow • gradually faster or slower • short/detached (staccato) • smooth/connected (legato) • accent
Melody	A succession of pitches that move up, down, or repeat	• high/low • up/down • steps/skips/repeated pitches
Rhythm	The long and short durations of sounds/silences and the organizations of these sounds/silences in time	• beat • long/short • pattern • beat groupings (two, three)
Form	The structure of a musical composition; the order of same/different musical events	• echo • call and response • same/different sections • same/different phrases
Texture **Harmony**	The layering of sound; the thickness or thinness of music Two or more pitches sounded simultaneously—the vertical structure of music (one aspect of texture)	• accompaniment/ no accompaniment • thick/thin • ostinato/drone

When writing a lesson plan that focuses on an element or a concept, teaching it using three different learning modes at some point during the lesson can work well. For example, if students are exploring loud and soft in a lesson, this could involve providing a listening example (Haydn's *Surprise Symphony*); showing movement that represents large movement for loud and small movements for soft; and finally, teaching the labels of *p* and *f* for soft and loud, and holding up a card that shows *p* or *f* when students hear the correct dynamic. Cards might include Braille for students with vision loss. If stereo speakers are on the floor and shoes are removed, students with hearing loss (and typical students) will feel the vibrations of dynamics better through the floor. Hard floors work best! Balloons with a small bit of rice inside may also be used to feel the vibrations when the balloon is held up to a speaker.

UDL lessons provide multiple ways for students to experience a concept, and teachers will often find that most students are naturally included without extra add-ons to a lesson. Experiencing music through activity before it is labeled (sound before symbol) will make students more successful. Children learn to speak before learning to read and write. Similarly, with music, people do better if they sing, play instruments, dance, or improvise before reading and writing music notation.

Experiences do not have to happen the same way for all children to learn. If a student with a physical disability is able to play a glockenspiel part at the end of phrases, but a crossover bordun part on the bass xylophone is difficult to master, it should be fine if he or she participates according to ability. If a student with a communication disorder cannot sing but can push a button that sings for her, then that should be acceptable as well.

Picture Exchange Communication System (PECS)

Special educators use the Picture Exchange Communication System (PECS) to assist students who have communication disabilities but are able to point to pictures to communicate their choices, needs, and answers to questions. A software program that most special educators use to create PECS is Boardmaker. Paraprofessionals can create PECS for use in the classroom. Some examples are shown below.

Play Keyboard

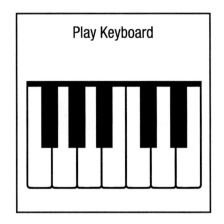

Play Ukulele

Play Orff

Play Drums

Compose

Improvise

Listen to Music

Read Notation

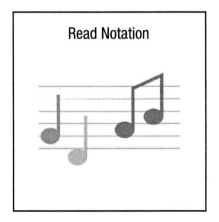

Move to Music

Conduct

Students on the autism spectrum handle transitions to activities better when PECS are used to organize the lesson. These are placed on a board with Velcro and can be torn off when an activity is completed, or virtual ones can be made and removed on a Smartboard™.

This one uses images for non-readers.

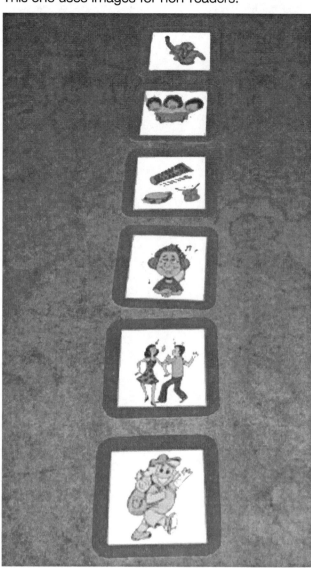

First Then, an iPhone/iPad™ app, is another way to create PECS. A Smartboard™ can be hooked up to an iPad™ to show routines created in the app for the class. These are particularly important to develop when preparing for a concert or a field trip. The routines can be rehearsed in the special education classroom, and, after rehearsing what to expect several times for at least a week, students will do better when the event comes.

Assistive Technology (AT)

This is the legal definition of assistive technology as described in the Individuals with Disabilities Education Act (IDEA) update in 2004:

Any item, piece of equipment, or product system, whether acquired commercially off the shelf, modified, or customized, that is used to increase, maintain, or improve the functional capabilities of children with disabilities.

The term does not include a medical device that is surgically implanted or the replacement of such device. (Authority 20 U.S.C. 1401(1))

Music teachers can receive federal funds to purchase devices or services if it is written in a child's IEP. The IEP team must be persuaded that the device, service, or instrument is needed to help the student fully access the music curriculum. There are literally thousands of devices available, and occupational therapists and music repairpersons can also help to make customized devices for specific students. If an item is purchased, it goes with the student to whatever school he or she attends, so it does not become something that stays in the music room.

Many instruments, stands, and electronic software can be used as AT. For example, an adjustable Orff instrument stand helps to bring the instrument closer to a student in a walker or wheelchair. The stand is needed in order for the child to access the music curriculum if Orff instruments have been placed on the floor.

A variety of commercially made mallets can be purchased to help students with physical disabilities access Orff instruments. Students who use T-grip controls for their electric wheelchairs can use T-grip mallets with success.

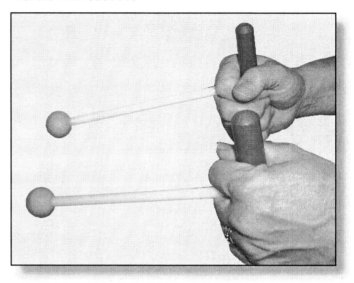

Mallets are made with heads that grip the bars better than yarn or plastic-head mallets. Some of these have grooved rubber or cork mallet heads. Often the grip is shorter and built up to accommodate students who have problems holding thinner, lighter, and longer mallets. However, some students do not like the way these sound and prefer to play with traditional mallets or mallets made for young children that are shorter.

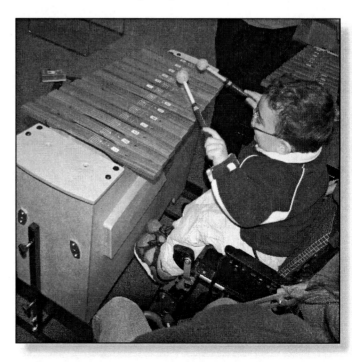

Kindermallets are shorter mallets. The mallet on the left is a Kindermallet.

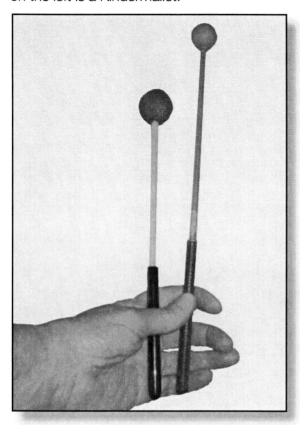

Traditional contrabass bar mallets are hard to control for students with physical and vision disabilities. A shorter version is made and sounds just as good as the longer mallet.

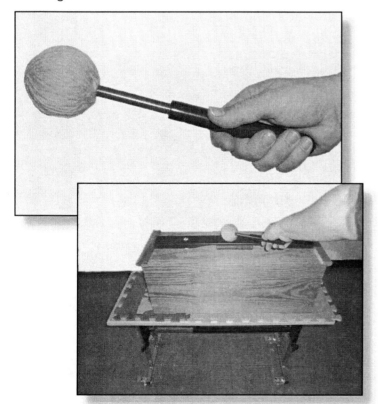

Mallet cuffs are adjustable Velcro straps that a mallet can be tucked into. Only the traditional mallets fit into the commercially available cuffs and can be awkward to manipulate with them.

Finger stix are sawed off tips of wooden drumsticks. These are slipped over the student's fingertips and stay on with an elastic band. They are light and easy to use. The photo below is a student with blindness who uses them for better control when playing the glockenspiel. Be aware that some students do not like the feel of the elastic on their fingers.

Tubano drums come in three sizes and work well for students who tend to hit hard. If the desired sound should be softer than what is typically played by a student, using these customized covers, called Not So Loud caps, can soften the sound. Remo makes these as well as drums that come with removable heads that include Not So Loud drumheads.

Jingle bells on a Velcro strap used to be the only accessible instrument for children with physical disabilities.

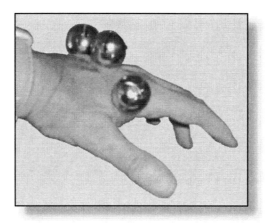

Jingle bells are fine for certain festive songs, but they are not appropriate for most other songs and can be tiresome to play if that is the only choice of instrument. There are now shakers and other small percussion that use elastic straps. This gives the student more options, although teachers should watch for students who don't like the feel of the strap on their hands.

Here is another way that might be more comfortable for students to play jingle bells. This is a soft, cotton-knit glove with bells sewn on the fingertips.

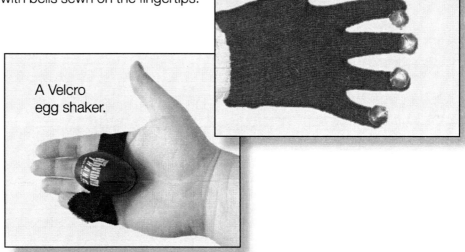

A Velcro egg shaker.

Students who struggle with holding non-pitched percussion instruments benefit from an instrument mount. This AT device has places for a number of different instruments.

An adaptive recorder is made by Aulos for students with missing fingers or fingers that need a different angle. This recorder can be customized and glued together to make an instrument that works better for the student. Unfortunately, customized recorders also have custom fingering charts. Group instruction might be confusing unless there are opportunities to work with individual students.

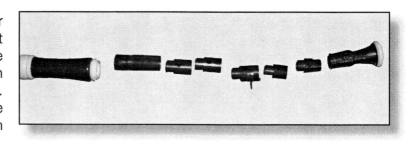

Occupational therapists can build and adapt devices for individual student needs. This piano chorder is a great example.

A student with good head mobility plays instruments with a mallet fastened to her baseball cap.

Drums that stay on wheelchair trays and tables have built-in rubber feet to keep them from moving. Rubber carpet mats work well, too.

Electronic Instruments and iPad™ Apps

Some of these instruments and apps offer extraordinary solutions for students with a variety of disabilities. Drum controllers come in a variety of sizes and prices. Most have raised rubber pads that are pressure sensitive. The grooves between the pads help orient students with vision loss and learning disabilities. The pressure-sensitive pads are terrific for students with very weak muscle movement. It can be so satisfying to barely tap one of these pads and produce a timpani roll!

Bigger pads help students with movement challenges. This controller can be programmed to play xylophone pitches, and the student can play ostinati and join his or her class.

This controller, made by Korg, fits with a small laptop. It works nicely as an input device when composing with a laptop. There is a touch screen for creating effects, too.

Some controllers use sounds from the computer and are less expensive. This one is placed on top of some of the non-slip material called Dycem. Carpet pads work well for this, too.

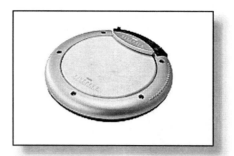

The Korg *Wavedrum* uses built-in sounds and works well for students who tend to hit hard. Some sounds are different, depending on how hard the *Wavedrum* is played or where the drumhead is hit.

The *Skoog* is a soft cube with raised foam buttons that plugs into a laptop computer. The *Skoog* software enables the device to play pitches or recorded sequences when pushing a foam button. The buttons are programmable and can be adjusted for sensitivity; a child with weak muscle control can lightly tap a button and get the *Skoog* to respond. The instrument can be programmed to play recorder sounds. Students who need an alternative way to play recorder with the class might have success using a *Skoog*. It is also washable.

The Soundbeam is an electronic instrument that responds to movement. It uses MIDI sounds that can be customized to single sounds or chords. The instrument can be programmed to play dozens of different scales in all keys by moving close to and away from the sensor. The newest version includes a sampler. A student who has no ability to vocalize can sing with her eyebrows using the sampled voice of her teacher!

The *Soundbeam* can also be accessed with switches. Switches can operate computers and many electronic devices.

The Korg *Kaossilator* is a small, hand-held device that can be operated using a touch pad. Sounds can be recorded and looped with options for keys and scales.

The *Makey Makey* can turn anything into a pentatonic scale by connecting its clips to any object and then to a laptop computer. It can also be used to create custom switches that can be operated by any moving body part. A demo video is at http://www.youtube.com/watch?v=rfQqh7iCcOU

Banana Piano

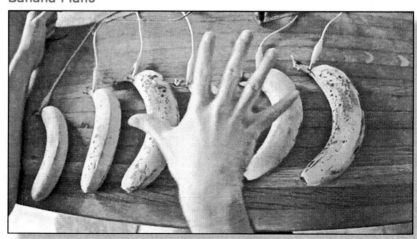

Switches and Buttons

Explore various types of switches and buttons to activate sounds and phrases that are recorded ahead of time. For example, if a lesson is about ABA form, the theme for the A and B sections could be recorded on two different buttons, and a student could demonstrate ABA form for the rest of the class.

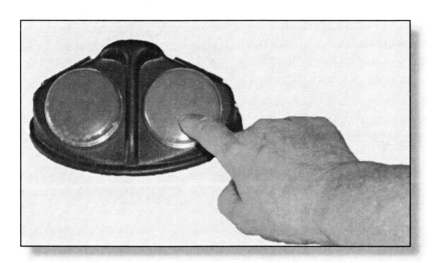

PVC Pipe Amplifier

Students who need to hear themselves better can use this simple device made from PVC pipe to hold to their ears while singing.

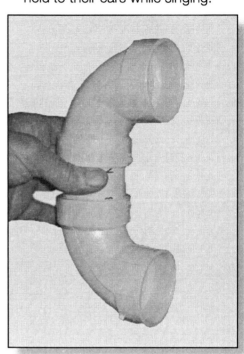

iPad™ Apps
Adaptive Use Musical Instruments (AUMI)

Adaptive Use Musical Instruments (AUMI) is free software available for Windows or Macintosh computers (and also as an iPad/iPhone app for a small charge). AUMI works by sensing movement and responding by playing programmable pitches or drum sounds. For example, if an eyebrow is where a student has the best control of movement, AUMI can be programmed to respond to eyebrow movement. The computer outfitted with a camera displays the individual's head, and in cross-hairs on the screen the eyebrow is in the center. A virtual piano keyboard can be used that appears as an overlay on the computer screen, or the screen can be split in halves or quarters and sounds programmed in each of the sections.

deeplistening.org/site/content/aumipadhome

EAMIR Note

A composing program designed specifically for children with autism. Controls are intuitive and limited, and built-in sounds are selected with sensory-defensive children in mind. Compositions can be recorded and saved. Lesson plans for using the app are available on the EAMIR website.

Programs that provide visual, aural, and tactile stimulation are inherently UDL. Many of these work very well for children who have difficulty moving from music class to another subject or who have frequent meltdowns. www.eamir.org/

Bloom

Bloom is an intuitive instrument that responds to touch by playing and sound, and by creating a visual that looks like colored drops falling in water. It is an excellent composition program for students with intellectual disabilities and students on the autism spectrum. It also works well as a musical transition. http://www.generativemusic.com/bloom.html

MeMoves

MeMoves is another excellent musical transition program. Children follow the path on the screen with their fingers while they listen to music. http://thinkingmoves.com/memovesapp.html

Singing Fingers

This program is designed to record the voice while the student draws on the screen. Once the song is saved, it can be played back by tracing the path. http://singingfingers.com/

Bebot

Bebot is an animated robot that sings with synthesized sounds. Pitch can be controlled by sliding a finger across his body. http://www.normalware.com/

Falling Stars

Falling Stars is a composition program that allows the student to draw in leaves and branches that catch falling stars. When the stars hit them, they make sounds according to how high a leaf or branch is drawn on the screen. http://www.tridentvitalitygum.com/fallingstars/

Pitch Painter

Created by composer Morton Subotnick, *Pitch Painter* is an excellent composing program that has been kid-tested by music educators. The program allows the user to "paint" pitches that appear as durations and pitches, much like piano roll notation. Music can be recorded and listened to later. http://www.creatingmusic.com/2012/pitchpainter.html

Music Sparkles

Children can select virtual instruments to play and choose other instruments to jam along with in *Music Sparkles*. http://learnbig.com/Resource?id=14710

Toca Band

Toca Band is an app that features student-selected ostinati that can be layered. This is a wonderful composing device, and if the student improvises, it can be a wonderful vehicle for self-expression. http://tocaboca.com/game/toca-band/

AirVox

AirVox allows the user to create gesture-controlled music that is similar to a Theremin. http://www.yonac.com/AirVox/index.html

MadPad HD

By importing video taken from an iPad™ or a Smartphone, *MadPad HD* allows the user to create compositions of found sounds, vocal sounds, or anything imaginable. http://www.smule.com/madpad

GarageBand

Chords can be altered and/or taken away in Smart instruments so students only see the chords they need to play.

Virtual Instruments

Playing virtual instruments allows a student to have control over volume and pitch. Students who are sensitive to volume and pitch can control their sound and hear it on headphones if desired. Having instruments that respond predictably allows children to be less hesitant about playing.

Triangle

The triangle is one instrument that can be irritating to students sensitive to high pitches. The instrument just has to be tapped to play it. It is easier to control as well, and the volume can be turned down!

https://itunes.apple.com/us/app/itriangle-free-virtual-triangle/id339143333?mt=8

Percussions

This app allows the user to choose from 18 different percussion instruments and to play it with a finger. The sounds are excellent.

http://www.crimsontech.jp/eng/percussions/

Recorder+ Lite

By clicking on the music staff, the user can hear and see the pitch, and the fingering instantly shows, too. The fingering chart might be a little confusing for some students to interpret, but the program can help provide instant instruction.

http://www.appszoom.com/iphone-apps/music/recorder-lite_dyvtd.html

Marimba

Soprano, alto, and bass Orff xylophones are realistically displayed with record and playback buttons.

http://itunes.apple.com/us/app/marimba/ld313056938

Guitar HD

This is an excellent-sounding guitar app with buttons to push to select chords. Chords can be strummed from low to high, or high to low, or the user can even play one string at a time.

https://itunes.apple.com/us/app/guitar!-hd/id434815760?mt=8

Korg iKaossilator

This virtual version of the handheld device on page 62 works similarly. Students can improvise and compose with one finger.

https://itunes.apple.com/us/app/korg-ikaossilator/id452559831?mt=8

Special Education Apps

ShowMe

ShowMe is a virtual whiteboard to create tutorials. This would be an excellent app to help prepare students for what to expect at concerts and field trips, and many types of short tutorials can be created to help children remember routines.

http://www.showme.com/

Sign 4 Me

This app is the perfect aid for learning short words and phrases in American Sign Language. If a student needs an interpreter in the classroom, the teacher can also use this app to learn some signs and better connect with the student. For example, "sing with us" or "play the hand drum" can be easily learned using this app. The app animates the sign, and it can be viewed from the front and from the side.

http://www.signingapp.com/sign4me_desktop.html

Stories2Learn

Social stories help students with autism learn how to interact socially. *Stories2Learn* lets the user insert photographs and record a narration to accompany the photos. For example, if a teacher wants to create a story about what happens when the class does movement, the first photo one might show how to do the movement, the second might show students being partnered together, the third may be of them holding hands, and so on.

http://vignettes.stories2learn.com/guide.php

Join.me

This app enables a student to see the Smartboard™ on the iPad™ or a Smartphone. Students with vision loss benefit from being able to enlarge the images that the rest of the class sees on the Smartboard™.

https://join.me/

Seat Cushions

Students with ADHD or sensory integration disorder often have trouble sitting in chairs for long periods of time or need stimulation. There are a variety of seat cushions that can be used with a chair or on the floor and that provide enough stimulation to help students focus better in class. In general, students with disabilities need chairs that aren't too big or small, so their feet touch the floor. Being grounded to the floor helps.

Sounding Board

Similar to a PECS board, this app allows one to set up small images to represent words or phrases. One can then record the word or phrase so that when a student touches the image, they can "speak" the word or phrase. This can be used for communication and to allow nonverbal students to sing along with the class by having them use someone else's voice that they can trigger with the images.

Holding Instruments

The following photos show what it looks like from the child's perspective to hold different instruments. This can help teach students who have trouble spatially reversing what is modeled to them by teachers.

Boomwhackers™

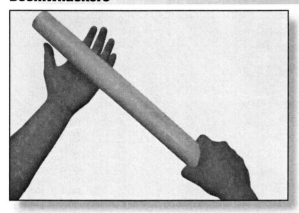 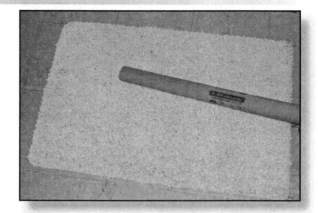

| **Cabasa** | **Chiquitas** |

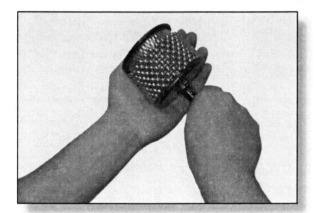 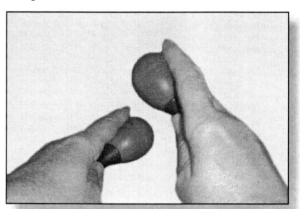

Claves

This adapted clave holder helps to maintain a proper grip without muting the clave.

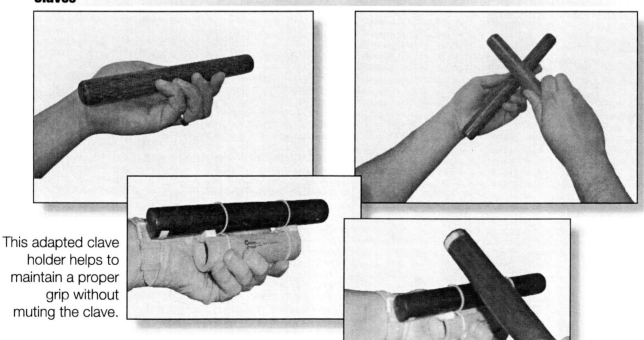

Cow Bell

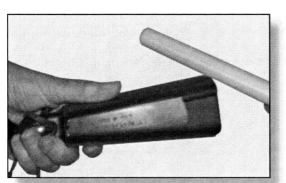

Cymbal

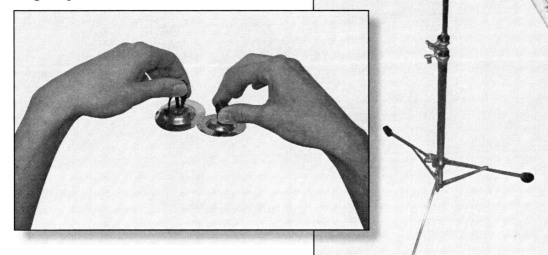

Finger Cymbals

Guiro

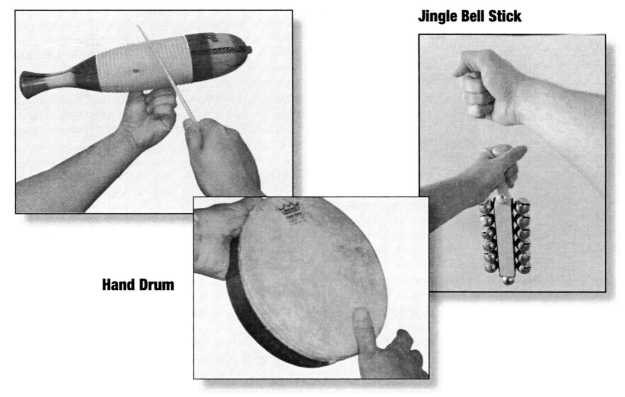

Jingle Bell Stick

Hand Drum

Maraca

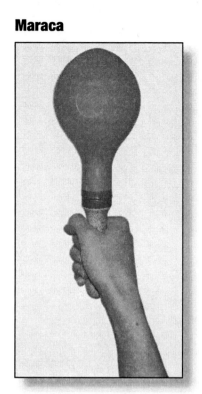

Ocean Drum

Rain Stick

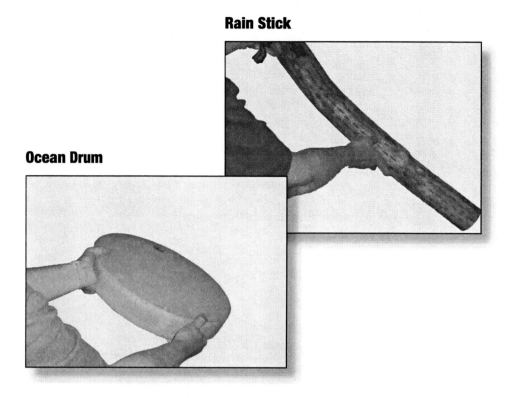

Holding the Recorder

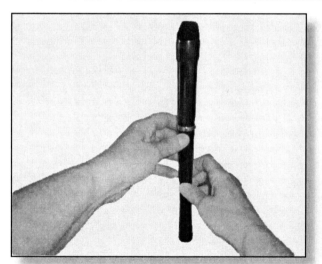

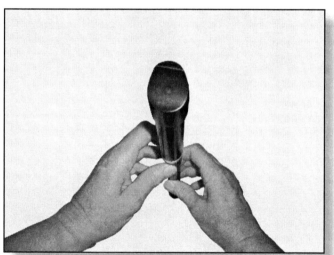

Rhythm Sticks

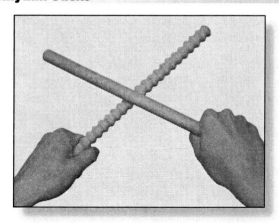

A smaller length of rhythm sticks is helpful for students with weak muscle control.

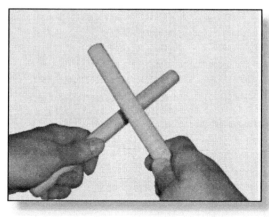

Sand Blocks

Shekere

Tambourine

Tambourine with Head

Triangle

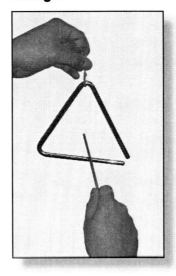

Wood Block

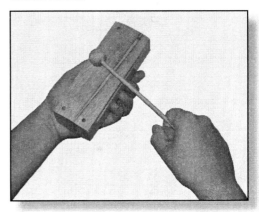

Instruments with Two or More Pitches

Agogo Bells

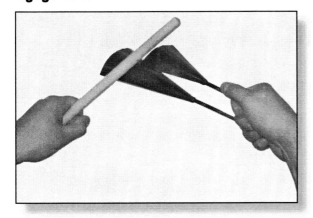

Bongos

Low

High

Log Drum

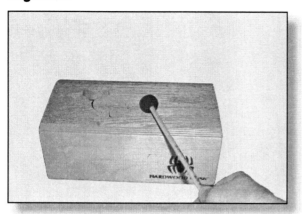

Piccolo Blocks

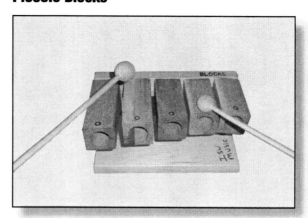

Temple Blocks

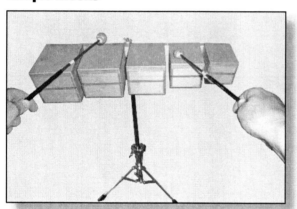

Tick Tock Block

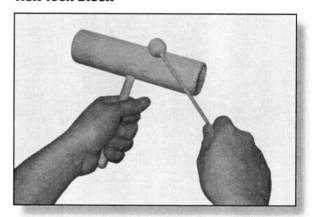

Tubano

A high sound is played with a closed palm on the edge of the drum.

A low sound is played with the heel of the hand slightly above the center of the drumhead.

Low

High

Students with weak muscle control can use these adaptive paddles to play tubanos.

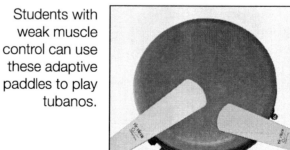

Assessment

UDL methods of assessment or other formal assessments are important to use occasionally in teaching. Below is a listening activity assessment developed by Kim McCord and Chicago Public Schools special educator Victoria Rollins. This assessment was used with autistic middle school students in a self-contained classroom. It shows different levels of assistance that might be used by the paraprofessional or the teacher.

	 Independent 5	 Touch Cue 4	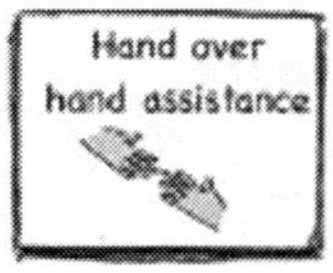 Hand over hand assistance 3
The student identifies the mood of the music by using word or picture support descriptors of what they hear in the recording.			
The student uses word or picture support descriptors to identify the composer's expressive intent.			

Student _____   Total _____

KEY

9–12 YOU'VE GOT IT!

5–8 Almost There

0–4 Keep Trying

A more detailed rubric was developed by special educators to be used by the paraprofessional assisting in the music classroom and features a prompting hierarchy that goes from full physical to independent. It is important to make a note if the student is having a bad day, because moods will likely impact ability to do well on a task (Floraday, E., Gandara, M., Kopke, M., Matschke, E., Truelson, and A., Valdez, H. 2013).

Rubric #1 Data Collection

Directions: Use the prompting hierarchy key below to score the student work product.
　　　　Begin with the least amount of support to assist the student with a task or skill.

Independent (no support needed)

Natural Cue (follow peers, transition when bell rings)

Gesture (number of cues needed: 1–2, 3–5, 6+)

Verbal (number of cues needed: 1–2, 3–5, 6+)

Visual/Picture (sequence steps of task for reference)

Model (teacher, paraprofessional, student/peer)

Partial Physical (hold paper when student is cutting with scissors)

Full Physical (hand-over-hand)

Task/Skill	Support (Refer to prompting hierarchy key)	Was the student able to demonstrate the skill when support was provided?	
		Yes	No

Additional Comments:

Student is having a good/bad day. Student works well with certain peers and/or staff. Student is affected by environmental factors. Student showed growth/regression on a specific skill. Student has some health concerns.

Rubric #2

Directions: Use the scoring tool below to score the student work product. After scoring student work, add points together to get a final student score 0–3 as determined by score ranges in the standards-based rubric.

	Insufficient Response 0	Developing 1	Proficient 2	Advanced 3
Task/Skill	No response	2–3 Higher-Level Prompts (Model, Partial Physical, Full Physical)	2–3 Lower-Level Prompts (Gesture, Verbal, Visual/ Picture)	Independent (Natural Cue)

Recording Students

Smartphones make wonderful handheld recorders. It is now easy to record or video tape students completing performance-based assessments and then listen or watch them later while filling out rubrics. Self/peer assessment is possible to complete using these recordings as well. Students with disabilities benefit from hearing how their peers assess themselves and others on specific tasks. Sometimes hearing a task explained or assessed in kid language by a peer helps students to understand how to complete a task better than when an adult explains or assesses it.

Getting to Know Your Students

It takes time to get to know students, and this becomes particularly hard when a student has a communication disorder. Special educators and paraprofessionals know the students with disabilities best and can provide information about them that will help customize the classroom for individual success.

Some students are easy to categorize as visual, aural, or kinesthetic learners. Students with hearing loss are going to rely on visual and kinesthetic/tactile systems to compensate for their lack of aural skills. Typical students—and students with disabilities that do not necessarily impact the senses—will be harder to categorize. When teaching a concept through all of the senses, asking students how many learned best when they were shown a picture, how many learned best when they performed movement, and how many learned best when they heard a song played on the piano can be effective. It will probably take several times of doing this to get a good idea of preferences. Some children will be combinations of two learning modes. Remember that teachers tend to teach mostly from their preferred learning mode.

Keeping a record of students' individual challenges can be helpful. It might look something like this:

Student Name	Visual	Aural	Record Students	Sensory Issues? Specifically	Trouble Reading Music?	Interests	Abilities
Jennifer		X		Vision loss	Yes, needs music enlarged	Likes to dance, hip-hop music, has a twin sister, two cats	Learning to read Braille, plays Orff instruments if bars are close together, sings, has perfect pitch
Scott			X	Yes, complains about lights buzzing (keep lights turned off); doesn't like being touched; wears noise-cancelling headphones	Doesn't look at music, participates best by echoing	Weather, likes to talk about weather channel shows, has a dog named Bear	Good memory for songs and routines

This is another form that aligns with the new Common Arts Standards by using the three artistic processes: creating (improvisation, arranging, and composing), performing (singing and playing instruments), responding (listening, evaluating music, and moving to music) and connecting (to other arts and other subjects).

Student Name_____ Date Observed_____

Assessing Abilities of Students with Disabilities in Music

Standard	Ability	Communication Requirements	Instrument	Interest	Adaptations	UDL Representation	UDL Expression	UDL Engagement
1. Singing: PERFORMING								
2. Playing instruments: PERFORMING								
3. Improvising: CREATING								
4. Arranging & Composing: CREATING								
5. Reading & notating music								
6. Listening & describing music: RESPONDING								
7. Evaluating music: RESPONDING								
8. Connecting to other arts & disciplines outside the arts: CONNECTING								
9. Understanding music in relationship to culture: CONNECTING								

Other Special Education Help and Professionals

Peer Helpers

There are always responsible students in classes who work well with students with disabilities. Other teachers have probably figured out that these same students make good peer helpers, and it might be that the helpers are weary of the responsibility of being the helper too much. It is good to ask if they mind being assigned as peer helpers first, before making an assignment.

Working with Paraprofessionals

Paraprofessionals are assigned to students with disabilities per their IEPs. If a paraprofessional is needed to accompany a student to music class, the IEP team should be written to with an explanation of why. If the team recommends that a paraprofessional come with a student or students, this will be written into the student's IEP. Sometimes a paraprofessional will accompany more than one student.

It is the job of music teachers to communicate with paraprofessionals about what they should do to assist students in music classes. Many paraprofessionals are nervous about music classes if they haven't had positive musical experiences themselves. They may need assurance that they won't need to sing or play instruments by themselves.

Some paraprofessionals need guidance about how much assistance to give students. Hand-over-hand assistance is sufficient to get a student started, but if it is done all of the time, the students never learn to make music themselves—the paraprofessional ends up making music for them. It should be clearly expressed to the paraprofessional that he or she isn't there to use the students' body to play instruments. Instead, assistive technology can help the student to be independent.

A checklist to help paraprofessionals know what they should do to assist music teachers in different activities can be really helpful. These can take some planning, but once most lessons have been developed, a collection will be available to use Loseke, D. (2013).

Lesson Plan: *Where the Wild Things Are* Unit—Music

Teacher will do:	Paraprofessional will do:
Lesson #1	**Lesson #1**
☐ Give the Anticipatory Set—read *Where the Wild Things Are.*	☐ Prior to the lesson, the paraprofessional will make copies of the worksheet for the rap/chant and gather materials in preparation for the lesson.
☐ Provide a statement of purpose and input on the lesson.	☐ While the teacher is instructing, the paraprofessional will monitor behaviors and re-direct when necessary.
☐ Provide a model and guided practice using describing words and emotions.	☐ The paraprofessional will move around the classroom assisting students (following the prompting hierarchy) on how to complete the rap/chant, re-iterating teacher language regarding describing words and emotions.
☐ Play the recording and model the rap/chant.	
☐ Provide guiding practice on writing the rap/chant using describing words and emotions.	
☐ Put students in pairs and walk around the room to assist students with writing the rap/chant.	☐ The paraprofessional will monitor behaviors and re-direct as necessary while students are performing their rap/chant.
☐ Have students perform the rap.	☐ The paraprofessional will collect worksheets.
☐ Provide closure to the lesson.	☐ The paraprofessional will gather materials and clean up.
Lesson #2	**Lesson #2**
☐ Give anticipatory set—read *Where the Wild Things Are.*	☐ Prior to lesson, the paraprofessional will make copies of the worksheet and gather and set out materials.
☐ Provide a statement of purpose and input on the lesson.	☐ While the teacher is instructing, the paraprofessional will monitor behaviors and re-direct when necessary.
☐ Provide a model and guided practice on feelings and moods.	☐ The paraprofessional will assist students/or individual students (following the prompting hierarchy) on how to write, draw, act, move, or show describing words, and re-iterate teacher language regarding feelings and moods.
☐ Play the recording and talk about describing words and how they match the music.	
☐ Provide a model and guided practice on how to write, draw, act, and move to show describing words.	
☐ Walk around the room and assist students as they write, draw, act, and move.	☐ The paraprofessional will collect worksheets.
☐ Provide closure to the lesson and have students complete a self-assessment.	☐ The paraprofessional will assist students as they complete their self-assessments (using the prompting hierarchy).
	☐ The paraprofessional will gather materials and clean up.

Working with Special Educators

Special educators can be terrific resources for music teachers when planning UDL lessons. It is likely they are already using some strategies to help their students in other subjects that can easily be transferred to music.

Uncertainty about which students have disabilities is possible; legally diagnosed disability does not have to be shared with all teachers. Knowing who has an IEP and what goals, objectives, accommodations, and adaptations are listed for the student isn't necessary. If this information is unavailable, special educators may be able to share this information. They are incredibly busy people, but most have a passion for helping their students be successful and will appreciate the effort.

Leaving a stack of these letters in their mailboxes at the beginning of the year is another successful option. These letters may be tweaked to include all the possible behaviors and skills expected during the year. These are a few possibilities to consider:

Dear Special Educator,

I want to let you know that I am interested in meeting the needs of students with disabilities in my music classes. I thought it might be helpful for you to know the types of skills and behaviors expected in my class, so you could advise me how I can best adapt for students with disabilities. You can return this checklist for each student that you have permission to do so. Please make a separate copy with recommendations for accommodations for each student. Thank you for all your hard work on behalf of kids at our school.

Respectfully,

Music Educator

☐ General Music   ☐ Band   ☐ Strings   ☐ Choir   ☐ Other

Student's Name_____

Particular Skills/Behaviors Needed	Your Suggestions for Accommodations
Movement with legs, arms, and hands	
Sing	
Read music notation	
Read lyrics/text	
Play instruments with one hand	
Play instruments with two hands	
Play instruments that require holes to be covered with fingers	
Play instruments that require physical support	
Play instruments softly and loudly (varied physical force)	
Play instruments that require articulating with tongue	

Play instruments that require hearing exact pitch	
March in the marching band while playing an instrument	
Perform movement while singing	
Read music in very small print	
Play an instrument that requires good lung capacity	
Listen to music and hear a variety of things, including volume, tempo, sounds in high, middle, and low range, different types of sounds, and durations of sound	
Listen to music with headphones on	
Work in collaborative pairs or small groups	
Attend after-school rehearsals or concerts	
Sight-read music under pressure	
Wear uniforms or choir robes	
Remember to bring instrument home to practice, and bring it back to school for class	
Ability to sit in one place for an hour or more	
Ability to focus for an hour or more	
Ability to take direction from the teacher and students who may lead the ensemble or sections of the ensemble	
Ability to take care of school-owned instruments and other property	
Ability to see from different locations in the room, stage, or on a field	
Ability to memorize music	
Ability to write	
Other	

Special educators can also help with assistive technology. In each state, there is a central office for assistive technology. Able Data (http://www.abledata.com/abledata.cfm) provides a list of all the thousands of assistive technology products and a list of the state AT centers. Many centers have lending programs. For example, if a student needs a seat cushion, several different ones can be tried before the one that works the best for the classroom and the student is chosen. It can then be requested in the IEP so that the product can be purchased.

Special educators can also be the connections to occupational, speech, and physical therapists. For an evaluation of what products, devices, or therapies

are available to help students function in a music class, a therapist may be requested to come to the class to observe both the student and the teacher.

Special educators are usually very familiar with the families of students, and they can answer questions about what to expect when contacting a parent or guardian. Parents appreciate knowing that a teacher cares, and parents especially value communications that are positive. Often the parent only receives negative communication about how much trouble their child is, but music can be one place where a child is successful. Letting the parent know can really brighten the day for a student and his or her family.

Concerts

Performances can be very anxiety provoking for children with disabilities. Rehearsing in the concert space and practicing entrances, exits, and behavior on the stage can prepare them for what to expect. Some children need to be reminded that the performance space will look somewhat different with people sitting and looking at them, that there will be applause, and how to acknowledge applause. Students with severe disabilities may have never attended a concert.

The considerations for making concerts UDL-friendly are numerous. In addition to students with hearing

loss, there may be audience members with hearing loss. Hiring an interpreter could encourage community members who may not regularly go to concerts with hearing loss to attend. The interpreter should be given lyrics to songs at least two weeks in advance and allowed time to rehearse with students.

Schools for the deaf or blind and senior citizens also often miss out on concerts. Making sure performance spaces are wheelchair accessible can allow them to be invited, as they appreciate being included.

Websites

Able Data
http://www.abledata.com/abledata.cfm

Search this massive database of thousands of assistive technology devices.

Children with Exceptionalities Special Research Interest Group
https://sites.google.com/site/exceptionalitiessrig/

This is an excellent resource for the NAfME group devoted to students with disabilities. Don't let the word "research" throw you! Check out "Resources for All" on the menu and find everything from films about people with disabilities to recently published dissertations about music education and disability.

Center for Applied Special Technology (CAST)
http://www.cast.org/

The most important website for UDL, CAST also hosts the book *Teaching Every Student in the Digital Age*.

Council for Exceptional Children
http://www.cec.sped.org/

The professional organization for special educators. Subscribe to the electronic newsletter and stay up-to-date on changes in special education law, assistive technology, and news on children with disabilities including music.

The University of Texas at Austin Center for Music Learning
Disabilities Information
http://cml.music.utexas.edu/online-resources/disabilities-information/introduction/

An excellent collection of information connected to specific disabilities and music.

DREAMMS for Kids
http://www.dreamms.org/

A free service for parents and teachers to find technology-based solutions for children with disabilities.

National Dissemination Center for Children with Disabilities
http://nichcy.org

Great information for early childhood and disabilities.

The Prism Project
http://prismproject.iweb.bsu.edu/

Ball State University's project to create concerts and events for children with disabilities.

Books

Adamek, Mary S. and Darrow, Alice-Ann. *Music in Special Education*. 2nd ed. Silver Spring, MD: American Music Therapy Association, Inc., 2010.

Atterbury, Betty Wilson. *Mainstreaming Exceptional Learners in Music*. Englewood Cliffs, NJ: Prentice Hall, 1990.

Clark, Cynthia and Chadwick, Donna. *Clinically Adapted Instruments for the Multiply Handicapped: A Sourcebook*. St. Louis, MO: Magnamusic-Baton, 1980.

Elliot, Barbara. *Guide to the Selection of Musical Instruments with Respect to Physical Ability and Disability*. St. Louis, MO: Magnamusic-Baton, 1982.

Hammel, Alice and Hourigan, Ryan. *Teaching Music to Students with Special Needs: A Label-Free Approach*. New York, NY: Oxford University Press, 2011.

Hammel, Alice and Hourigan, Ryan. *Teaching Music to Students with Autism*. New York, NY: Oxford University Press, 2013.

Jacquiss, Victoria and Paterson, Diane. *Meeting SEN in the Curriculum: Music*. London, UK: David Fulton Publishers, 2005.

Lazar, Michelle and Jensen, Jeremy. *Tuned in Learning: Music and Multimedia Resources for Special Education*. San Diego, CA: Tuned in to Learning, 2005.

Miles, Tim, Westcombe, John, and Ditchfield, Diana. *Music and Dyslexia: A Positive Approach*. 2nd ed. West Sussex, England: Wiley, 2008.

MENC: The National Association for Music Education. *Spotlight on Making Music with Special Learners: Selected Articles from State MEA Journals*. Lanham, MD: R&L Education, 2004.

Ott, Pamela. *Music for Special Kids: Musical Activities, Songs, Instruments, and Resources*. Philadelphia: Jessica Kingsley Publishers, 2011.

Rose, David H. and Meyer, Anne. *Teaching Every Student in the Digital Age: Universal Design for Learning*. Alexandria, VA: ASCD, 2002.

Salmon, Shirley, ed. *Hearing, Feeling, Playing: Music and Movement with Hard-of-Hearing and Deaf Children*. Wiesbaden, Germany: Reichert Verlag, 2008.

Schraer-Joiner, Lyn E. *Music for Children with Hearing Loss: A Resource for Parents and Teachers*. Oxford University Press, 2014.

Journals

Approaches: Music Therapy & Special Music Education
http://approaches.primarymusic.gr/

An online journal in English and Greek.

General Music Today
http://gmt.sagepub.com/

An online publication of NAfME. Each issue includes an article focused on general music and disability.

Journal of Music Therapy
The official journal for the American Music Therapy Association.

Organizations

American Music Therapy Association
http://www.musictherapy.org/

Council for Exceptional Children
https://www.cec.sped.org/

International Society for Music Education
http://www.isme.org/

An international music education organization with the Commission of Music in Special Education, Music Therapy and Music Medicine.

National Association for Music Education (formerly MENC)
http://www.nafme.org/

Includes the Special Research Interest Group for Children with Exceptionalities.

VSA John F. Kennedy Center for the Performing Arts
http://www.kennedy-center.org/education/vsa/

International organization for children and adults with disabilities in the arts. The Kennedy Center holds regular conferences that include many sessions devoted to UDL. Grants and state organizations are part of the many programs VSA hosts.

Author Bios

Amy Gruben received her Bachelor of Music Education degree from University of Illinois, Urbana-Champaign and her Master's degree in Music Education from Northwestern University. Amy has more than seven years of teaching experience at the middle-school level. She currently teaches choral and general music at Wood Dale Junior High School in Wood Dale, IL.

Kimberly McCord is Professor of Music Education at Illinois State University. She is the past chair of the ISME Commission on Music in Special Education, Music Therapy and Music Medicine and the founder and past chair of the National Association for Music Education Special Research Interest Group on Children with Exceptionalities. Her research focuses on music assistive technology, collaboration between music and special educators, and jazz and improvisational thinking in children.

Jesse Rathgeber is currently a Ph.D. student in Music Education at Arizona State University. Prior to this, Jesse taught K–5 general music at Kildeer Countryside School District 96 and K–12 music at DeLand-Weldon Community Unit School District 57, both in Illinois. Jesse received his Bachelor of Music Education degree from the University of Illinois at Urbana-Champaign and his Master's degree in Music Education from Northwestern University. His research interests include composition, creativity, and special-needs music education.

Appendices

Appendix A: Adapted Notation Examples

Note: For students who have difficulty reading, changing the background color of the paper can help them differentiate graphic elements more easily.

Hey, Ho, Nobody Home

Hey, Ho, Nobody Home

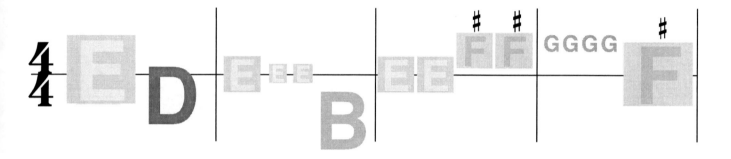

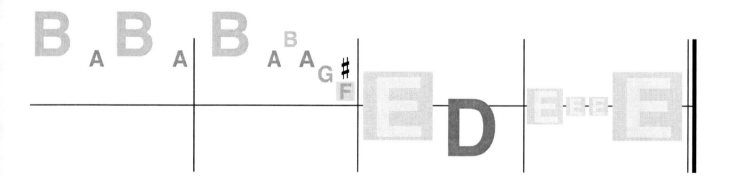

Lapka, C. (2006). Students with disabilities in high school band:"We can do it!". *Music Educators Journal*, 92(4), 105-106.

Hey, Ho, Nobody Home

Hey, Ho, Nobody Home

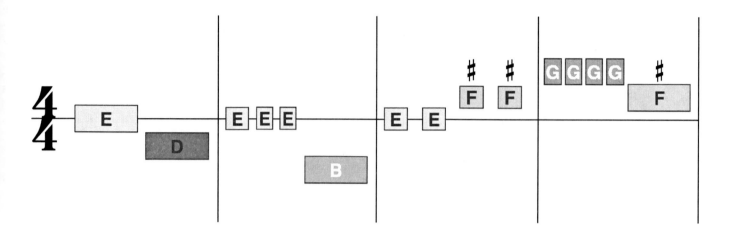

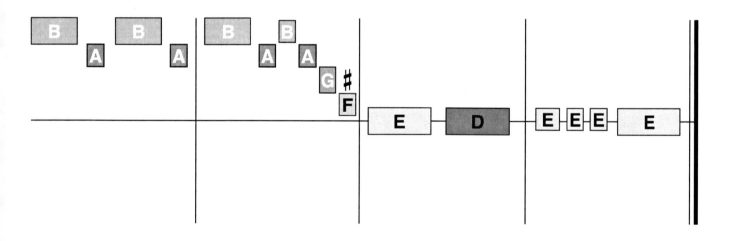

Hey, Ho, Nobody Home

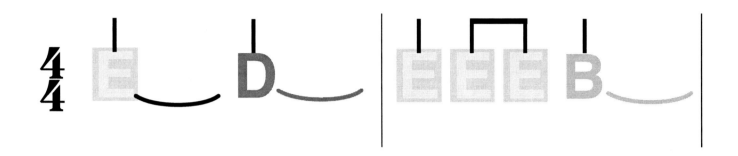

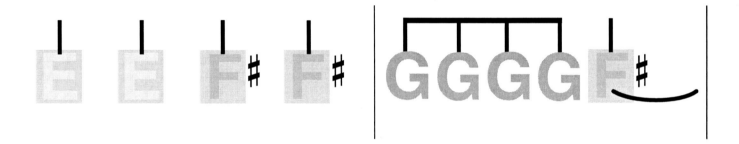

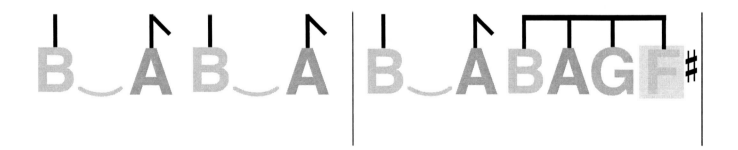

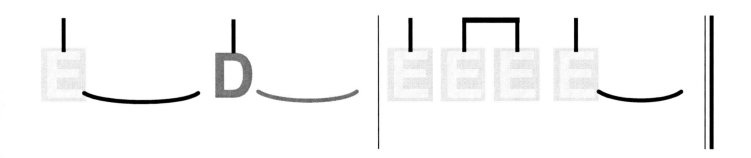

Twinkle, Twinkle, Little Star

Twinkle, Twinkle, Little Star

Lapka, C. (2006). Students with disabilities in high school band:"We can do it!". *Music Educators Journal*, 92(4), 105-106.

Twinkle, Twinkle, Little Star

Twinkle, Twinkle, Little Star

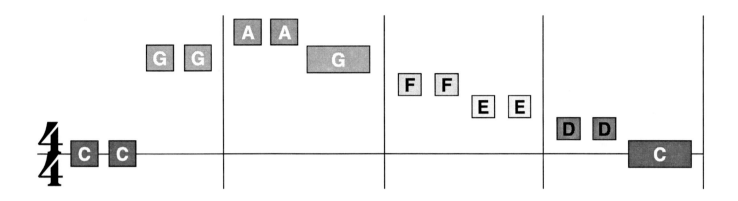

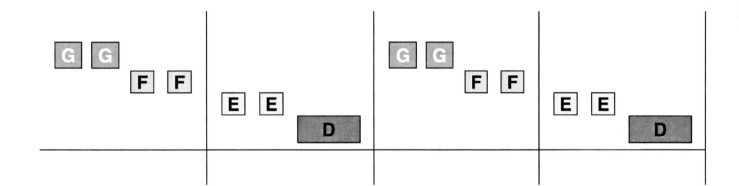

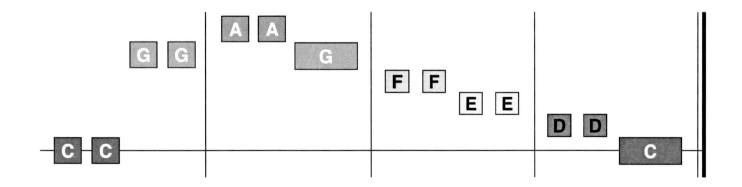

Twinkle, Twinkle, Little Star

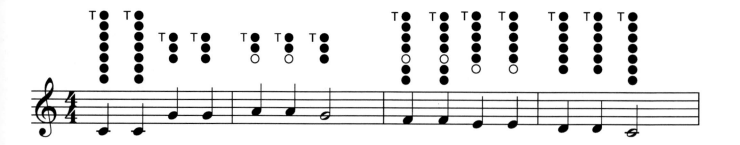

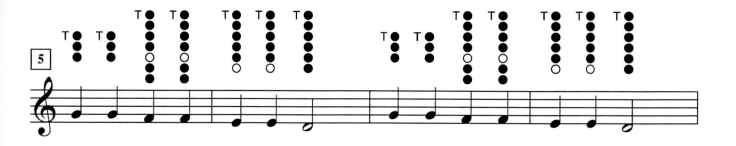

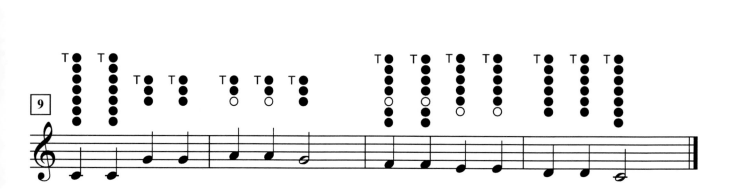

Twinkle, Twinkle, Little Star

Twinkle, Twinkle, Little Star

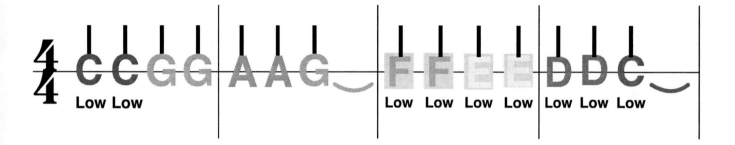

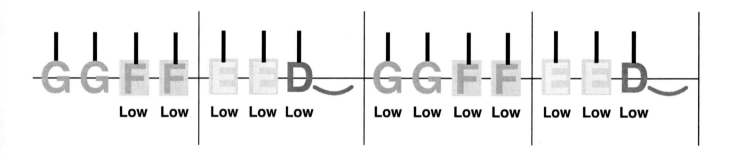

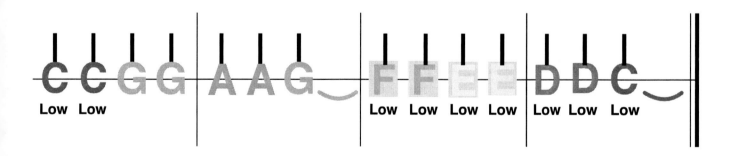

Yankee Doodle

Yankee Doodle

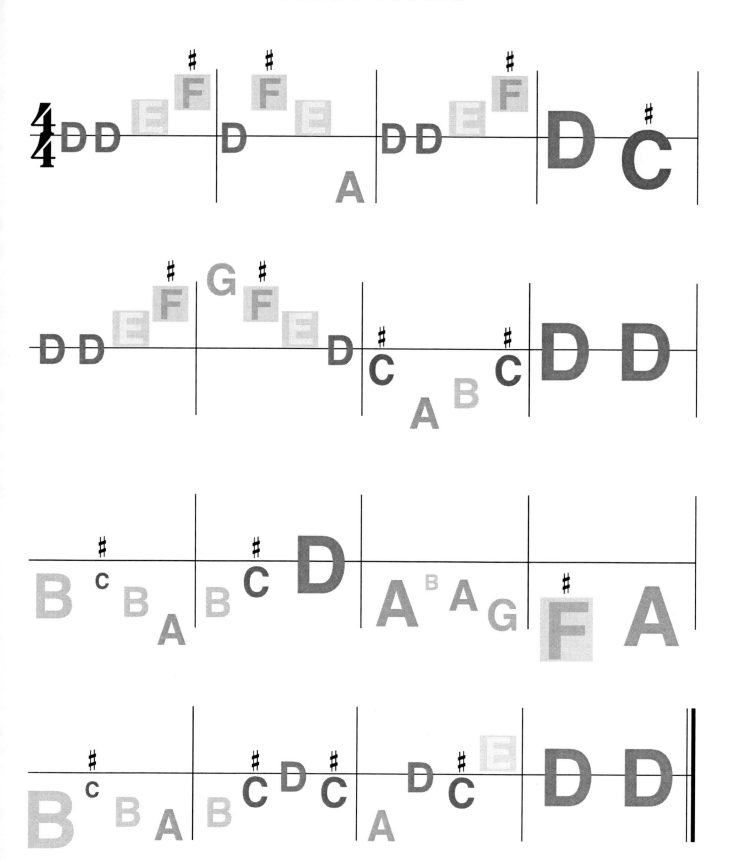

Lapka, C. (2006). Students with disabilities in high school band:"We can do it!". *Music Educators Journal*, 92(4), 105-106.

Yankee Doodle

Yankee Doodle

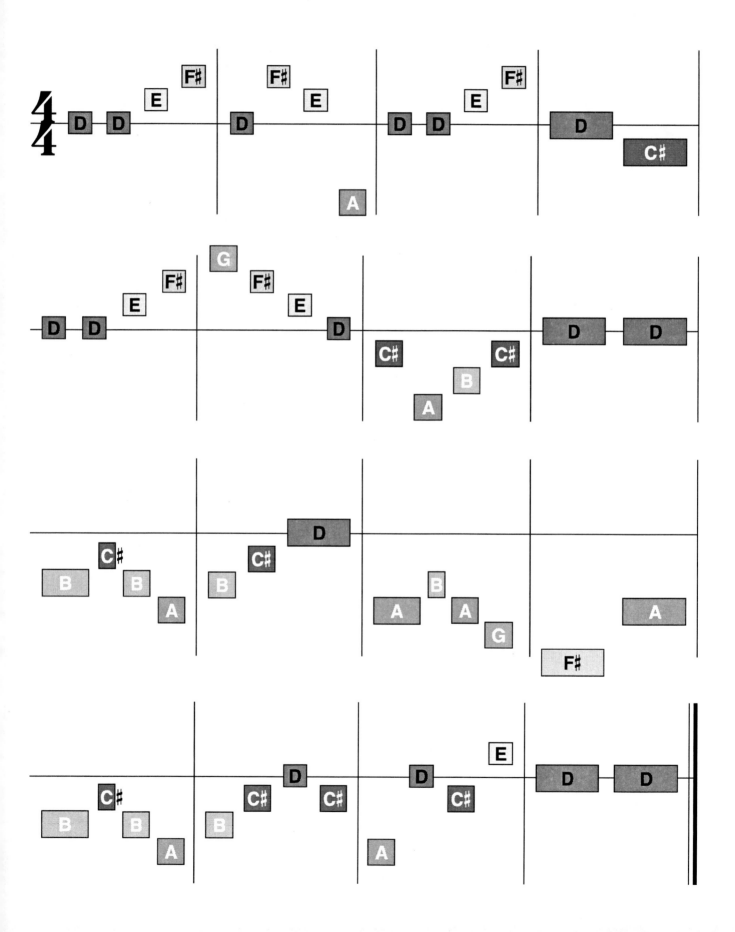

Yankee Doodle

Amazing Grace

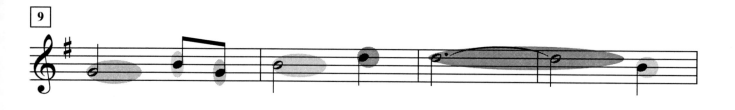

Amazing Grace

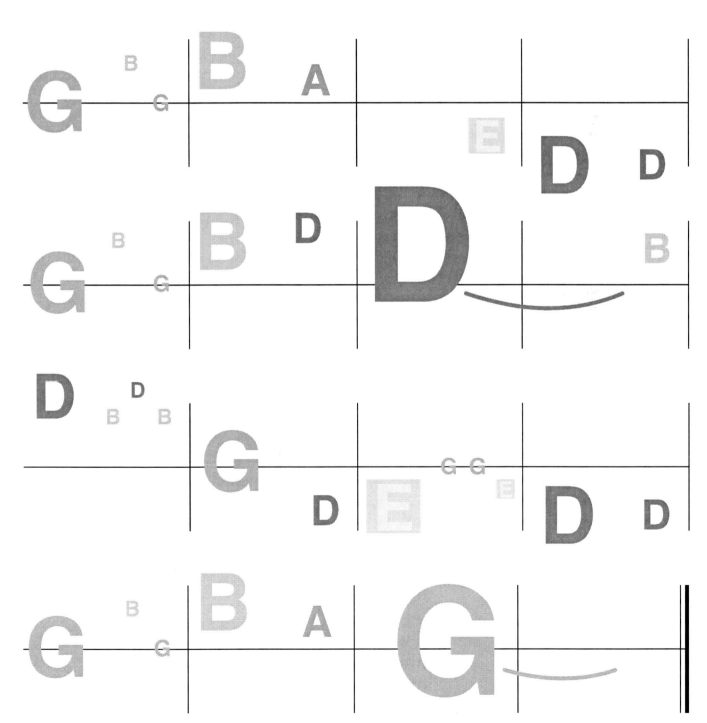

Amazing Grace

Amazing Grace

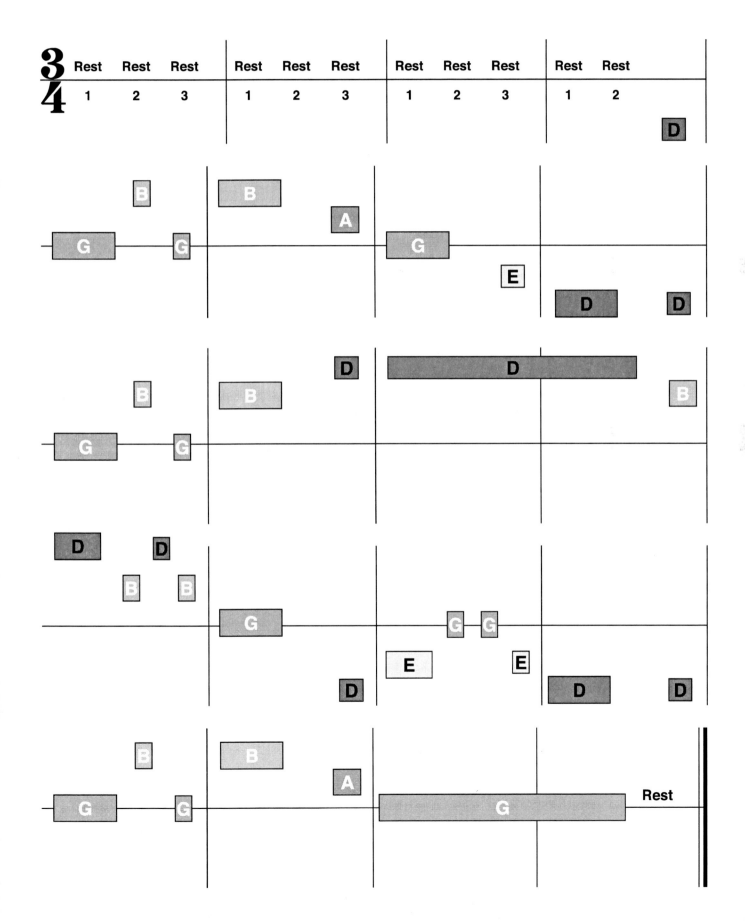

Amazing Grace

Amazing Grace

Amazing Grace

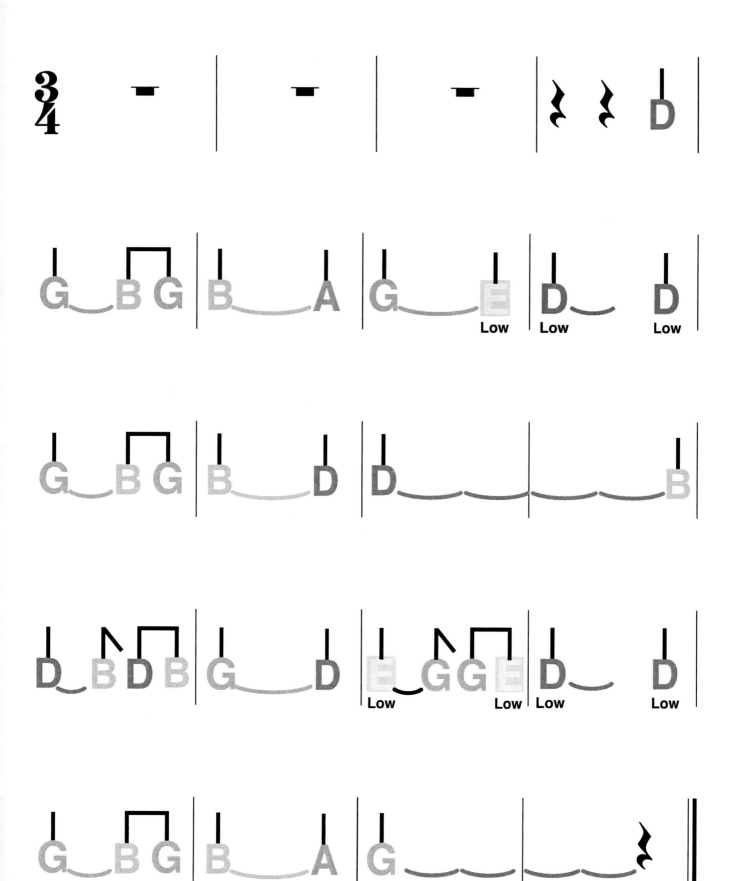

Appendix B: Keyboard Examples

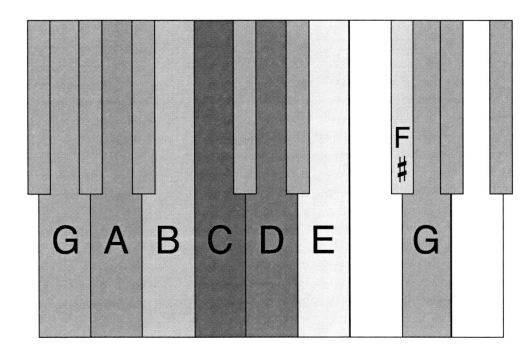

Key of G

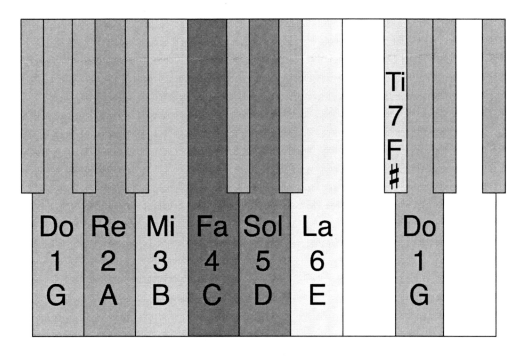

Key of G

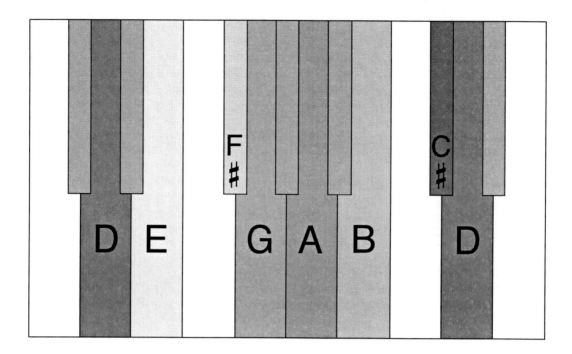

Key of D

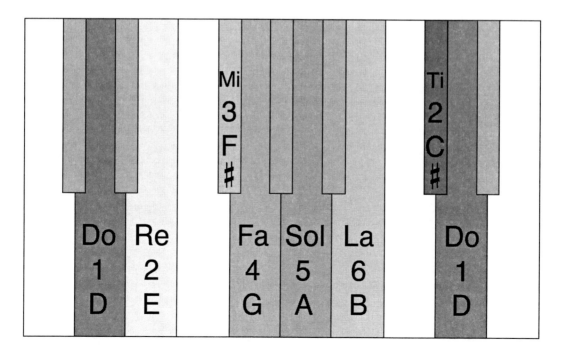

Key of D

Appendix C: Tablature Examples

Hey, Ho, Nobody Home

Standard Notation

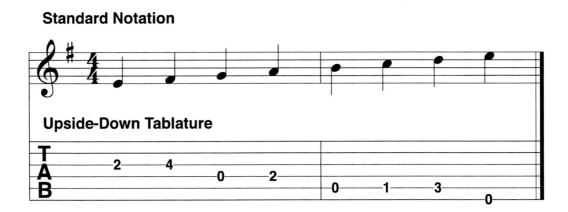

Upside-Down Tablature

Guitar

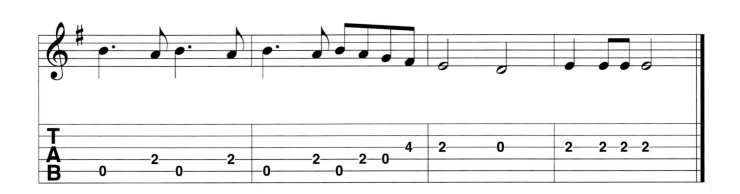

Hey, Ho, Nobody Home

Standard Notation

Upside-Down Tablature

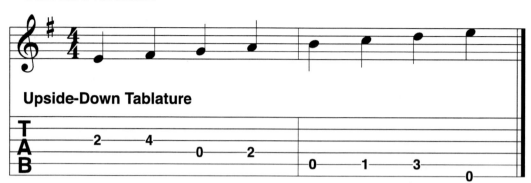

Guitar

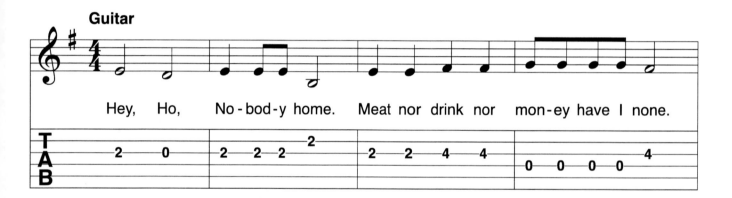

Hey, Ho, No-bod-y home. Meat nor drink nor mon-ey have I none.

Yet will I be mer - ry! Hey, Ho, No-bod-y home.

Twinkle, Twinkle, Little Star

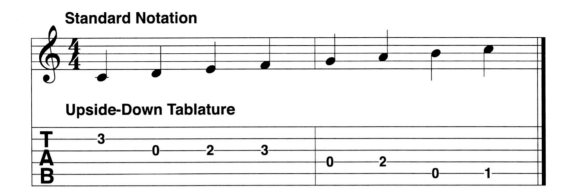

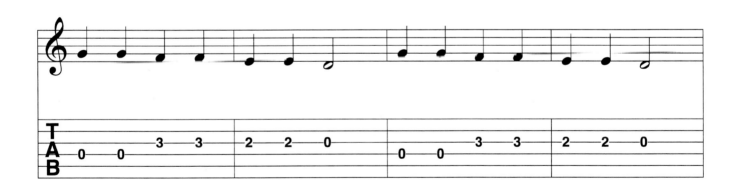

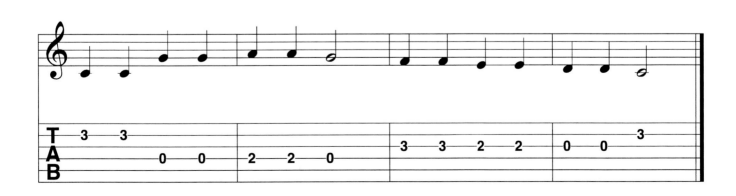

Twinkle, Twinkle, Little Star

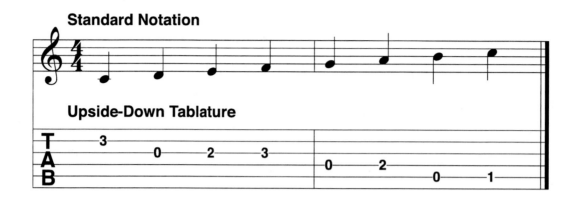

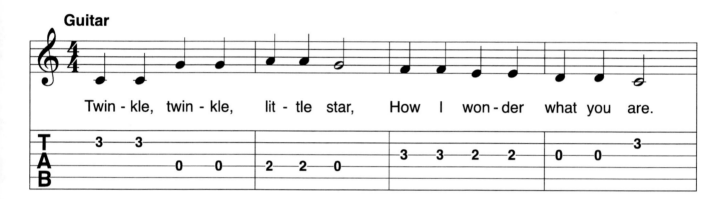

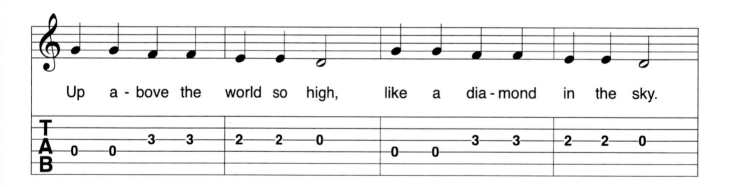

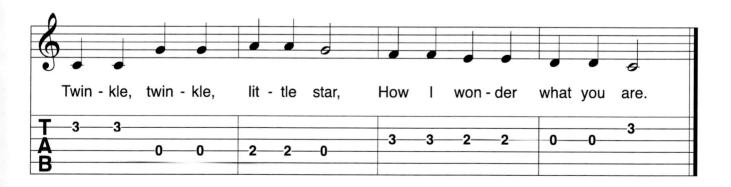

Yankee Doodle

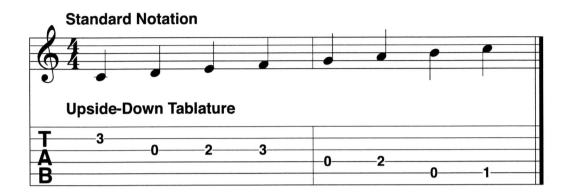

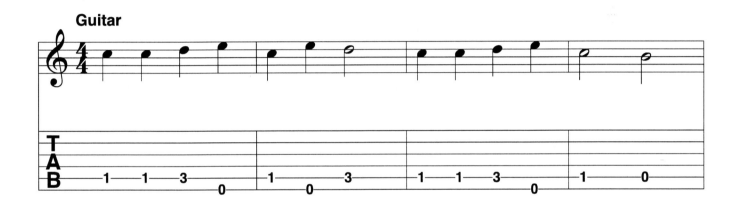

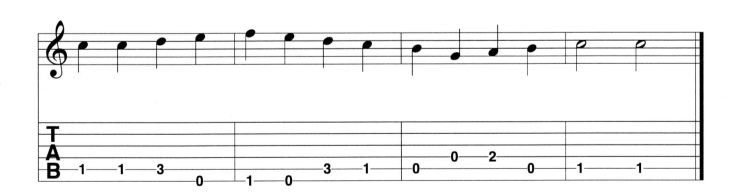

Yankee Doodle

Standard Notation

Upside-Down Tablature

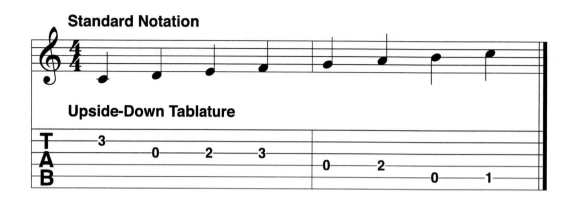

Guitar

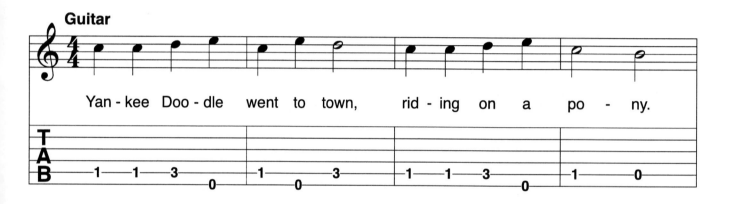

Yan - kee Doo - dle   went to town,   rid - ing on a   po - ny.

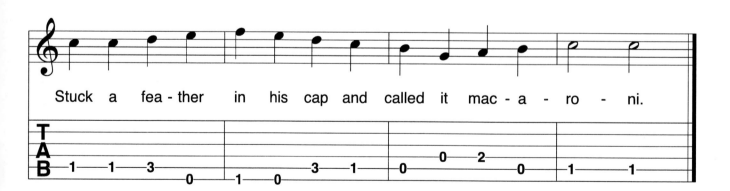

Stuck a fea - ther   in his cap and called it mac - a - ro - ni.

Amazing Grace

John Newton

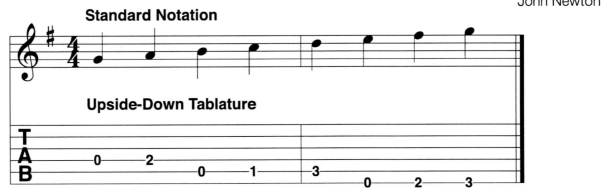

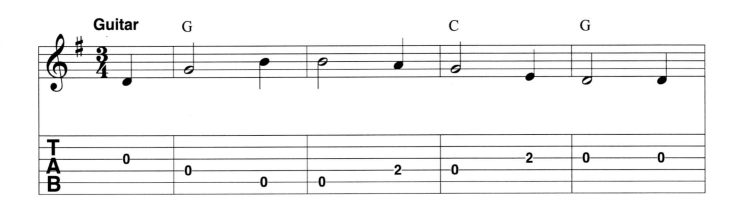

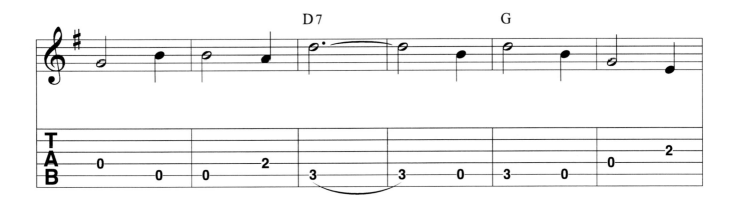

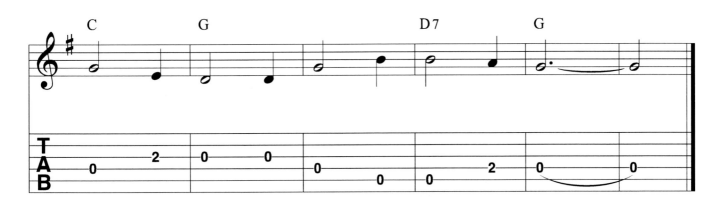

Amazing Grace

John Newton

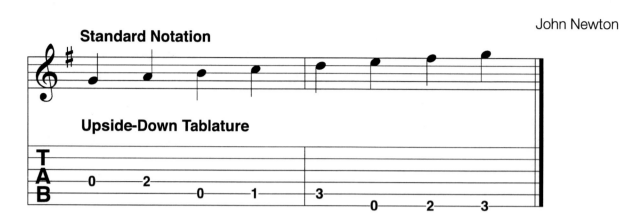

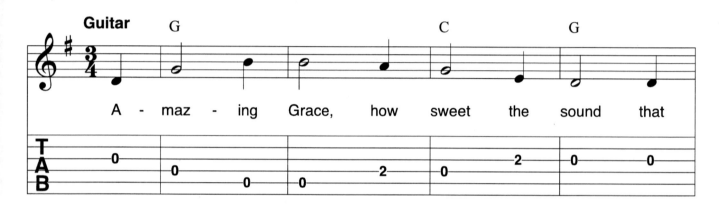

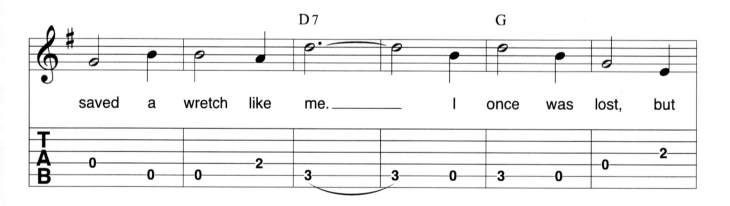

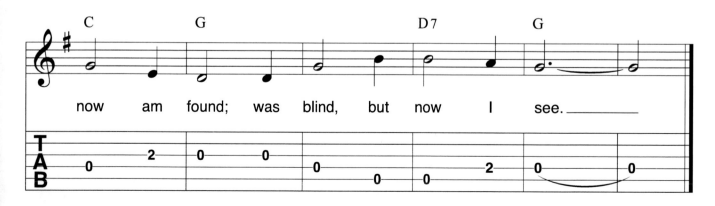

NOTES

NOTES